PHYSICAL EDUCATION

The profession

PHYSICAL EDUCATION

THE PROFESSION

JANET B. PARKS, D.A.

Associate Professor, School of Health, Physical Education, and Recreation, Bowling Green State University, Bowling Green, Ohio

with 38 illustrations

The C. V. Mosby Company

ST. LOUIS • TORONTO • LONDON   1980

To **David and Clara Frances Parks**
. . . with Love

Copyright © 1980 by The C. V. Mosby Company

Printed in the United States of America

The C. V. Mosby Company
11830 Westline Industrial Drive, St. Louis, Missouri 63141

Library of Congress Cataloging in Publication Data

Parks, Janet B   1942-
   Physical education, the profession.

   Includes bibliographical references and index.
   1. Physical education and training.
I. Title.
GV341.P29   613.7   79-24507
ISBN 0-8016-3759-7

VT/M/M 9 8 7 6 5 4 3 2   01/A/065

Preface

Orientation to physical education has proved to be a source of great dissatisfaction and concern for many individuals involved with the professional preparation of undergraduate, majoring students. Primarily, problems have arisen with respect to the amount of information that students can be expected to understand and apply within the framework of an introductory course. This book represents an effort to solve these problems.

The intent of this book is to introduce students to physical education—not to overwhelm them with dates, facts, figures, lists, and information that has taken professionals many years to accumulate and absorb. The topics of study are those that are revealed through articles published in *The Journal of Physical Education and Recreation, The Physical Educator,* and *Quest* between 1930 and 1979. Through an examination of the literature and subsequent class discussions of the topics, students will become acquainted with the ideas of physical educators, both past and present, and with many of the trends and issues that have been discussed and debated historically.

Physical educators frequently communicate ideas and share concerns through the medium of professional literature. An awareness of the available literature and an appreciation for the contributions that its contents can make to physical educators help them fulfill their obligations to their future students in an enlightened manner. With that objective in mind, the students who complete this course should exhibit the following behaviors relative to each of the professional topics considered in this book:

1. Identify professional organizations and publications.
2. Identify selected authors and personalities in the profession.
3. Conduct purposeful investigations of professional literature.
4. Identify and discuss selected professional trends and issues within historical and contemporary contexts.
5. Recognize and discuss similarities between concepts introduced by physical educators of the past and those promulgated by contemporary physical educators.
6. Recognize and interpret implications of traditional trends and issues for contemporary physical education programs.

v

7. Articulate personal rationales for electing to pursue physical education as a profession or for electing to focus career choices on other areas of endeavor.

These objectives will be reached through an examination of selected professional literature. The basic premise for this approach is that an investigation of this literature develops a genuine awareness of certain aspects of the profession. This approach assumes that we tend to relate more personally to the information presented in the articles than if we are simply *told* about it. In addition, the literature reveals that many contemporary trends and issues in physical education are not new. To generate the realization that significant professional concerns have existed for many years is an important educational purpose of this book.

The book consists of six chapters: (1) "Objectives of Physical Education," (2) "Elementary School Physical Education," (3) "Coeducation in Secondary School Physical Education," (4) "Competitive Athletics," (5) "Physical Education and the Special Child," and (6) "Career Opportunities." These topics were selected on the basis of their relevance to the physical education profession and their predicted significance for prospective physical educators.

Within each chapter are several reprinted articles pertinent to the topics under consideration. These articles are followed by extensive reading lists of additional pertinent articles. The articles are numbered consecutively within each chapter and are referred to by number in the assignments provided at the end of each chapter.

The articles selected for study are drawn from the three professional periodicals previously mentioned. There are, of course, numerous other publications containing articles pertinent to physical education. Some of these will be discovered through library research and should be incorporated in class studies. An introduction to the three aforementioned periodicals, however, will suffice as the initial step in developing an awareness of professional literature.

The Journal of Physical Education and Recreation, often referred to as *JOPER,* has borne several titles since 1930, among them *The Journal of Health and Physical Education; The Journal of the American Association for Health, Physical Education, and Recreation; The Journal;* and *Journal of Health, Physical Education, and Recreation.* Regardless of the title, this periodical continues to be the official publication of the national professional organization for physical educators at all levels of education. This organization also has had various names since 1930, including the American Physical Education Association; the American Association for Health, Physical Education, and Recreation; The American Alliance for Health, Physical Education, and Recreation; and the current name, the American Alliance for Health, Physical Education, Recreation, and Dance.

The Physical Educator, first published in 1940, is the publication of Phi Epsilon Kappa, a professional service organization in physical education.

Quest, initiated in 1963, was for many years published jointly by the National

Association for Physical Education of College Women and The National College Physical Education Association for Men. In 1978, these organizations combined to form The National Association for Physical Education in Higher Education (NAPEHE). Currently, *Quest* is the publication of NAPEHE.

Suggestions for individual activities and group presentations are given at the end of each chapter. The numbers associated with each assignment refer to the articles that contain information relative to that topic. Not every student is expected to undertake every assignment, but each student should participate in at least one group presentation. The instructor will determine which assignments will be completed.

Individual activities are intended to provide an understanding of various points of view expressed in the literature. They are designed to be used as the basis for independent research of the literature and subsequent class discussion or composition of written or oral reports.

For *group presentations,* students are not required to report on any one article but are expected to explore the topic and to present the essence of the information garnered through their reading. The group presentations are designed to involve class members in the topic under consideration through opportunities to research the literature and to present the information to the class. All students are encouraged to be creative and innovative in preparing these presentations. Costumes and props will enhance the effectiveness of the presentations and will produce more receptive and responsive audiences.

Physical Education: The Profession is presented with the hope that this approach to the orientation of prospective physical educators will enhance students' understanding of the profession. If the book serves its purpose, the result will be individuals who will participate with increased knowledge and awareness during subsequent courses and experiences in the professional preparation curriculum.

The photographs in this book were provided by Clifton Boutelle, Bowling Green State University Photo Service.

The completion of this book represents the fulfillment of a dream that could not have been realized without the assistance of many friends and professional colleagues. Therefore, sincere gratitude and appreciation are extended to: Dr. Glen P. Reeder, Middle Tennessee State University, for his enthusiasm, guidance, and creative contributions; Dr. Ralph B. Ballou, Jr., Middle Tennessee State University, for his valuable suggestions relative to composition, structure, and style; Dr. Donald A. Lau, Middle Tennessee State University, for his interest, attention, and suggestions; the authors who made their publications available for inclusion in this book; Dr. David Gallahue, Nancy Rosenberg, and Dr. Hope Smith, for their cooperation in securing reprint permission; Dr. Darrell Crase, Memphis State University, Dr. Helen Fant, Louisiana State University, Dr. Scott Greer, Indiana University, and Dr. Celeste Ulrich, University of North Carolina, Greensboro, for their critical assessments and constructive comments; and Dolores A. Black, Bowling Green State University, for her artistic assistance, encouragement, and support.

Finally, appreciation is expressed to the faculties of Girls' Preparatory School and the University of Chattanooga, Chattanooga, Tennessee; Illinois State University, Normal, Illinois; and Middle Tennessee State University, Murfreesboro, Tennessee for providing the educational foundation from which this book is derived.

Janet B. Parks

Contents

PHYSICAL EDUCATION

The profession

"The results of a good physical education are not limited to the body alone, but they extend to the soul itself."

Aristotle, 350 BC

CHAPTER ONE

Objectives of physical education

As you begin to explore the profession of physical education, you might want to ask yourself these questions: Why have I chosen physical education as the area that I wish to pursue as a career? What experiences have led me to this decision? Why do I feel that physical education is worthy of my time and effort? What are physical educators trying to accomplish?

No doubt, you have a concept of the nature of physical education and personal reasons for deciding to become a professional physical educator. You may not have given a lot of thought to *specific* purposes and objectives of physical education, but probably you have had experiences that have led you to believe in the value of physical activity. Chances are that you enjoy being involved in physical activity and that you have an interest in influencing others to develop skills in, and appreciations for, such involvement. Although these interests and appreciations are significant and vital, there are more complex considerations that you should take into account in order to begin building a stronger foundation for entering this challenging field. Foremost among these considerations is an understanding of basic reasons for the existence of the profession. In searching for these reasons, you must answer certain questions, such as: Why is physical education important? Does it contribute to the quality of life, and if so, what are its contributions? In what ways should students be changed by virtue of having received instruction in physical education? In other words, what are the *objectives* of physical education?

Although you could list numerous objectives of physical education, it may be astonishing to discover that physical educators have been debating this issue for decades. As a prospective physical educator, it is essential that you investigate the varying points of view and begin to establish personal convictions about the objectives of physical education. These convictions may be based on an acceptance of one particular school of thought or on a creative application of a combination of various points of view to your own concept of physical education. Regardless of your final decisions, the path leading to those conclusions should involve a thorough examination of the information available to you. The formulation of beliefs relative to the objectives of physical education requires intellectual curiosity,

1

serious thought, and a decided commitment to an investigation of the ideas and ideals of those physical educators who have shaped the past, the present, and the future of physical education.

Although physical education enjoys a heritage that dates back long before the twentieth century, the physical educators of the twenty-first century may be interested in fairly current opinions and arguments. Therefore, this chapter will be limited to discussions of ideas that have been promulgated by scholars who have published articles in professional literature since 1930. As you assimilate the in-

Golf can provide fun and satisfaction for a lifetime.

formation, you may notice that physical educators of the 1960s and 1970s espouse many of the same ideas as those of the 1930s and 1940s did and that current concepts of the objectives of physical education are strongly rooted in professional practices and societal trends of the past. The evolution of modern academic and social concepts is fascinating and may serve to enhance your appreciation of the foresight of the professionals who paved the way for the physical education of the 1980s.

An investigation of the literature published since 1930 reveals that there have been primarily three schools of thought relative to the objectives of physical education: (1) physical education as education through the physical; (2) physical education as education of the physical; and (3) physical education as education for human movement.

EDUCATION THROUGH THE PHYSICAL

Proponents of the *education through the physical* point of view support the thesis that physical education involves more far-reaching objectives than merely the development of the physical body. Rather, its goals extend to *total* education accomplished through the medium of physical activity. Basic to this concept is the idea that education of the *mind* may occur *through* the education of the body. With this thought in mind, the objectives of physical education become identical to the objectives of other curricular subjects, and the existence of physical education in the school setting can be justified.

The term *education through the physical* has enjoyed widespread popularity and for many years has been recognized as a basic tenet of physical education. Although the concept usually is interpreted in rather general terms, the scholars adhering to this school of thought differ somewhat in their viewpoints about the *specific* desired outcomes of physical education.

Jay B. Nash, a prominent physical educator and a prolific author, proposed four primary objectives for physical education:* (1) organic development (growth); (2) neuromuscular development (skills); (3) interpretive-cortical development (intelligence, insight); and (4) emotional-impulsive development (behavior). Nash's outlook became very popular, and several generations of physical educators became proficient in reciting his four basic objectives!

Jesse Feiring Williams, a professional colleague of Nash, also believed in educating the whole child through the medium of physical activity. Williams, in fact, coined the phrase *education through the physical*. He proposed that physical education should contribute to the development of:† (1) a complete, intensive, full

---

*Nash, J. B.: The administration of physical education, New York, 1931, A. S. Barnes & Co., Inc., p. 6.
†Williams, Jesse Feiring: A fundamental point of view in physical education, The Journal of Health and Physical Education 1:10-11, 60, January 1930.

life; (2) skill in leisure-time activities; and (3) proficiency in recreative activities. The idea of physical education as education for *life* was at the core of Williams's point of view.

Additional objectives that have been suggested by other proponents of the education through the physical point of view include: social development, moral development, intellectual development, development of physical and mental health, development of cooperation, reduction of juvenile crime, enrichment of

Racquetball—a popular leisure-time activity.

life, personal adjustment, and the development of the perfect human being. This list may appear to be exhaustive, but it does not represent all of the objectives of physical education that have been suggested by authors in this area.

Although their concepts of the specific desired outcomes of physical education may vary to some extent, the scholars espousing the education through the physical point of view agree that physical development, although an important objective, is inappropriate as the *sole* objective of physical education. The concomitant values achieved through physical education are of primary importance. The concept of the *totality* of the human being is the underlying premise on which the education through the physical school of thought is based.

EDUCATION OF THE PHYSICAL

According to C. H. McCloy, "the basis of all physical education—developmental, educational, corrective, or any other aspect of our field—is the adequate training and development of the body itself."* It was on this premise that the

---

*McCloy, C. H.: How about some muscle? The Journal of Health and Physical Education 7:303, May 1936.

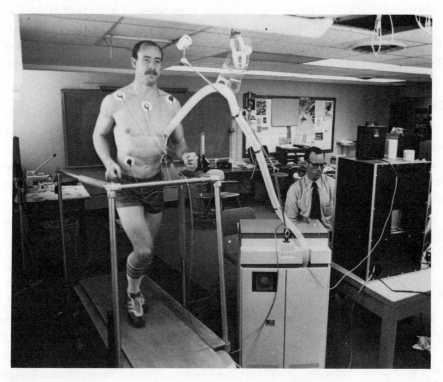

Cardiovascular efficiency is measured in a human performance laboratory.

pioneers of American physical education based their programs. In their opinions, physical education was justified as a curricular subject on the basis of its *unique physical* contribution to the education of the whole child, and the early programs included, primarily, exercises designed for physical training and development.

The proponents of this point of view maintain that the word *physical* is significant in the term *physical education*. These scholars contend that many of the social and cultural objectives proposed by the education through the physical school of thought may be attained through a physical education that emphasizes the training and discipline of the body. Development of the body, acquisition of biomechanical and physiological skills and abilities, and application of knowledge and habits *can* contribute to the development of character and personality. However, the emphasis must be on the physical aspects, which are unique to physical education, rather than on the concomitant benefits, which may be assumed desirable of any educational field regardless of area of specialization.

McCloy felt that many physical educators suffered from inferiority complexes about physical activity and development. He disdained the concept of the "great American intellect" and challenged physical educators to return to the basic purposes of physical education. Although the *education of the physical* school of thought was destined to be relatively short-lived during the twentieth century, modern physical education is experiencing somewhat of a revival of McCloy's attitude toward physical education's efforts to become unduly academic and intellectual. The most popular contemporary concept of physical education accords renewed respect to the notion that the word *physical* should take its rightful place in the definition of physical education.

EDUCATION FOR HUMAN MOVEMENT

The concept of physical education as *education for and through human movement* currently is generating the most discussion among physical educators. Although this concept is less easily described than the preceding viewpoints, Eleanor Metheny, a leader in the human movement approach, offers a commonly accepted definition:

> If we may define the *totally educated person* as one who has fully developed his ability to utilize constructively all of his potential capacities as a person in relation to the world in which he lives, then we may define the *physically educated person* as one who has fully developed the ability to utilize constructively all of his potential capacities for movement as a way of expressing, exploring, developing, and interpreting himself and his relationship to the world he lives in.*

Physical education as education for and through human movement, therefore, seeks many of the same educational goals as those earlier theories sought, but the

---

*Metheny, Eleanor: The third dimension in physical education, Journal of Health, Physical Education, and Recreation **25:**27, March 1954.

emphasis has shifted to the study of human movement as the unique mission of physical education. The human movement point of view has resulted in a new definition of physical education—a definition based on the concept of movement education as a lifelong process of which physical education is a component. "Physical education is that part of movement education which has been desig-

Weight training contributes to the development of physical strength.

Karate requires an understanding of human movement.

nated as a responsible, educational program (subject) in a school curriculum."* Bette J. Logsdon and associates, proponents of the human movement approach, express the goals of physical education as they reflect the psychomotor, the affective, and the cognitive domains of learning:

> Physical education should provide experiences that improve the ability of the learner to:
> 1. Move skillfully demonstrating versatile, effective, and efficient movement in situations requiring either planned or unplanned responses.
> 2. Become aware of the meaning, significance, feeling, and joy of movement both as a performer and as an observer.
> 3. Gain and apply the knowledge that governs human movement.†

The influence of the human movement approach is apparent in the position paper published in 1970 by the American Association for Health, Physical Education, and Recreation.

> Physical Education is that integral part of total education which contributes to the development of each individual through the natural medium of physical activity—human movement. It is a carefully planned sequence of learning experiences designed to fulfill the

---

*Logsdon, Bette J., and others: Physical education for children; a focus on the teaching process, Philadelphia, 1977, Lea & Febiger, p. 11.
†Ibid., p. 17.

growth, development, and behavior needs of each student. It encourages and assists each student to:

DEVELOP the skills of movement, the knowledge of how and why one moves, and the ways in which movement may be organized.

LEARN to move skillfully and effectively through exercise, games, sports, dance, and aquatics.

ENRICH his understanding of the concepts of space, time, and force related to movement.

EXPRESS culturally approved patterns of personal behavior and interpersonal relationships in and through games, sports, and dance.

CONDITION the heart, lungs, muscles, and other organic systems of the body to meet daily and emergency demands.

ACQUIRE an appreciation of and a respect for good physical condition (fitness), a functional posture, and a sense of personal well-being.

DEVELOP an interest and a desire to participate in lifetime recreational sports.*

The human movement approach to physical education, therefore, embraces portions of both of the earlier theories and molds them into yet another concept of physical education, based on the study of the science of human movement.

SUMMARY

An investigation of physical education literature reveals the fact that controversy exists relative to the objectives of physical education. The primary schools of thought are:

1. Physical education as education *through the physical*
2. Physical education as education *of the physical*
3. Physical education as education *for human movement*

These viewpoints are not self-contained and, indeed, overlap to some extent. They do, however, represent different emphases with respect to the content, processes, and outcomes of physical education programs.

Throughout the literature, proponents of each school of thought present convincing arguments supporting their positions. Determining which viewpoints to accept is frequently a difficult process for prospective physical educators. Decisions must be made, however, and objectives must be established for future students and programs. These objectives will, in turn, influence many aspects of those programs, including content, methodology, evaluation techniques, and student accomplishments. The adoption of personal convictions about the objectives of physical education represents the first step toward the development of programs based on principles, implemented with insight, and received with enthusiasm.

---

*American Association for Health, Physical Education, and Recreation: Guidelines for secondary school physical education, Washington, 1970, The Association, p. 4.

1   A FUNDAMENTAL POINT OF VIEW IN PHYSICAL EDUCATION*

By Jesse Feiring Williams, M.D.
Professor of Physical Education, Columbia University

Ideas of the time and place influence what people do in shipbuilding, in war, in art—in all the manifold activities that make up the life of the people concerned. Educational enterprises respond to the molding influence of dominant ideas and "every aspect of education must adjust itself to the national ideal."[1]

Some sixteen centuries ago organized physical education was planted—a slip from the wisdom of intellect and understanding. There on the shores of the Aegean Sea it grew into a sturdy plant to nourish the future citizens of a Greek City State. Its form was fashioned by the prevailing ideas and needs as revealed by the philosophers and statesmen of that period. Harmony, beauty, and courage were the ideas that guided the performances in the palestra.

Later in Rome a totally different notion prevailed. The training of youth on the Field of Mars reflected the aggressive, colonizing, war-like consciousness of Rome. Greek aesthetics were never quite understood; but military exercises with shield and spear, on the ground or on horseback seemed the great values.

In neither Athens nor in Rome was physical education destined to enjoy permanently a place of preference. Military conquest cheapened it; asceticism set up other practices in relation to other ideas.

Its role in modern European nations reflects accurately the compelling influences of nationalistic needs, purposes, and ideals. The kind of Germans desired by those in power a century ago was shaped in part by the kind of physical education established in the schools and universities of the Fatherland. The nationalistic needs of

Sweden are reflected in the plans for educational, military, and medical gymnastics devised by Ling and his co-workers. The early efforts in America in the Nineteenth Century vividly portray the ideas of the people regarding education, personal values, and national needs.

Assuming then that physical education may be viewed in relation to the dominant ideas of a people, let us ask, What are some of the prominent needs in American life to which physical education has something to contribute?

In the first place, American life is primarily an industrial life. Since 1880 the swing of the population has been constantly toward the cities so that the last census showed a majority of the population living in cities or towns of 25,000 inhabitants or more. The next census will continue this remarkable increase. The factory system has changed the American home and American life. Industry that was formerly carried on in the home providing developmental and training activities for the young has been taken advantageously into factories. The typical home varies from a few cells in an apartment house to a tidy bungalow with a narrow strip of lawn and backyard sufficient only for a clothesline and an ash can. This organization of society is the product of adult organization for economic gain. It has been possible under this impetus in less than one hundred and fifty years to have exploited tremendously our natural resources, to have reclaimed vast areas of untillable soil, to have stretched in all directions over 30,000 miles of railroads, to have builded great cities that house there the teeming millions of people.

Bogart, in describing phases of this remarkable economic advance states that "Generally, in all the western settlements, three classes, like the waves of an ocean, have rolled one after other." He pictures first the pioneer depending for subsistence upon crude agriculture and the proceeds of hunting. Next he portrays the more

---

*From The Journal of Health and Physical Education **1**:10-11, 60, January 1930.
[1]Russell, W. F.: School Administration and Conflicting American Ideals. Teachers College Record, October, 1929, p. 17.

permanent settler who purchases land and becomes an owner who clears the forests, builds roads and eventually mills and schoolhouses. Thus develops a plan and frugal type of civilized life. Bogart then concludes "Another wave rolls on. The men of capital and enterprise come. The settler is ready to sell out and take advantage of the rise in property, push further into the interior, and become himself a man of capital and enterprise in turn. The small village rises to a spacious town or city; substantial edifices of brick, extensive fields, orchards, gardens, colleges, and churches are seen."[2]

To make the picture complete he might have added: Soon appear jails, hospitals, sanitariums, clinics, reformatories, asylums, and other signs of man's failure to provide for essential biologic needs in the face of insistent economic demands.

The smug complacency of the past generation in its economic success is challenged again and again by those who have stopped long enough to ask: What's it all about? These critics are saying that unless living becomes increasingly more worth while, happier, kindlier, and unless man retains the power to enjoy, to play and to find pleasure therein, the economic gains scarcely are justified. To have wealth and not to know how to use it is a social loss; to have leisure and not to know how to use it, is an individual and social disaster.

A sincere skepticism of popular notions of progress have stimulated questioners to ask, "What is the chief end of man?" To an increasing degree the answer has had a biological slant—to function. "This answer has meant clearly that the purpose of life was to live, to live completely, intensively, fully; to function in every wholesome aspect of one's being."[3] *To the extent that physical education has anything to contribute to such living, this idea must shape and fashion its practice in a democracy.*

In the second place, our modern age is characterized by an enormous increase in leisure time. Less than ten years ago the Monthly Labor Review commented as follows: "It is rather a striking testimony, however, to the spread of the belief in a relatively short working day that over 3/5 of these employers had established a working week of forty-eight hours or less."[4] And again, "For skilled labor the eight-hour day as a standard seems to have been won and considerable progress appears to have been made toward securing a forty-four hour week."[5] Since then the progress has been rapid. In the fall of 1926, Henry Ford proposed a five-day week for his shops and today it is actually in operation. Moreover, the President of the American Federation of Labor announced that today three great basic industries are ready for the five-day week.

Now the increase of leisure time does not in itself guarantee richness and fullness of living. Some centuries ago those in power feared leisure time and indoctrinated the people with the idea that play was sinful, that happiness on earth was not to be expected. The old hymn still reads, "On the other side of Jordan, in the sweet fields of Eden,—there is rest for you." The modern world has clearly rejected crosses and although an ill-conceived life may still be a cross, the thoughtful of today are asking about education for leisure. *To the extent that physical education has anything to contribute to leisure time activities, this idea must shape and fashion its practice in a democracy.*

In the third place, our modern age exhibits a tremendous increase in commercialized amusement. On Saturday, October 26, 1929, it is estimated that over 800,000 persons watched football games. The popularity of professional baseball, pugilism, and hockey shows that people have leisure time and are interested in physical contests. It is a common observation of experienced physical education teachers that generally willingness and zeal to engage in an activity vary directly with the skill in the activity. A person who is a "dub" at tennis prefers to have a headache or an appointment with the dentist to an engagement on the courts. The exceptions to this rule, that participation and proficiency go together, are due to the belief in the hygienic values of exercise so that from time to time the adult novice ventures upon the links—but it is not a pleasurable experience, only a kind of mystic rite for the

[2]Bogart, E. L.: The Economic History of the United States. 3rd Ed. Longmans, Green and Company, 1920, p. 190.

[3]Williams, J. F.: Principles of Physical Education. W. B. Saunders Company, 1927, p. 214.

[4]Monthly Labor Review. U. S. Department of Labor, July, 1920, p. 97.

[5]Monthly Labor Review. U. S. Department of Labor, July, 1920, p. 99.

goddess Hygeia. *To the extent that physical education has anything to contribute to proficiency in recreative activities, this idea must shape and fashion its practice in a democracy.*

The fundamental point of view now offered holds that physical education of a kind has a great deal to contribute to fine and wholesome living, that it is essential to a sensible plan for leisure time education, and that it is indispensable in the education of people in important motor skills. These three ideas are intimately bound together and each reinforces the other. They do require, however, a careful analysis of kinds of physical education.

Within the memory of many and available to all in the literature of education, there was an idea that the purpose of education was to exercise the mind. Mental gymnastics were supposed to be good for one wholly aside from any consideration of the content used in the process. Fortunately education today is totally removed from any such benighted notion. Even the most conservative of the Liberal Arts Colleges today justify their classics at least in part by the contribution they are supposed to render to a richer and fuller life. The whole of professional education is directed toward functional utilities and the brain is trained in relation to the work to be done. It would be extremely difficult for anyone anywhere in the United States to secure a school for the purpose of exercising only the brains of students.

And yet, let us observe the extent to which this unwarranted idea prevails in the popular notions of physical education. The radio "physical director"—most appropriately named—leads countless thousands in exercise of the muscles, and schools and colleges set up programs, hire teachers, and lead children in exercises for the muscles. In the light of outstanding social needs and ideas it is just as unreasonable to propose physical education on an exercise basis as it would be to advocate courses in school to exercise the brain.

Clearly the purpose of physical education is to educate people to live more fully, more intensely, more finely. Instead of a technic acquired for esoteric or hygienic demands it is a way of life. Our political philosophy demands that this view be obtained, our growth in leisure time foreshadows its adoption, and our reliance upon proficiency for satisfaction guarantees its success. The boy or girl graduating from high school or college today, who is unacquainted with recreative skills that can bring joy to his living, occupation to his leisure, and satisfaction in his performances, is not educated for living fully. Examples of genius that can live without a physical education, only enforce the argument for the great mass of our population. Nor should the needs of physically illiterate adults and physically defective children be neglected. The former may still be offered setting-up exercises in a gymnasium or over the radio; the latter must always have the special services of the expert therapeutist.

Physical education as a way of living will provide exercise as a by-product of interesting and worthwhile recreations. Play, games, sport, and dancing will be engaged in because they are in themselves worth while, entirely sanctioned by an intelligent appreciation of wholesome living. We may hope to escape from the notion that play must be profitable, golf will not be played for health—a horrible use to which to put such a noble game—and games and dancing will be cherished as worthwhile in themselves precisely as are sitting in the sun, listening to music by the water, or walking in the garden in the twilight.

When Voltaire was attacked and insulted by the London mob, he stood on his door step and complimented them upon the nobleness of their national character, their glorious freedom, and their love of liberty. The London mob missed the sarcasm. When those responsible set up programs of physical exercises to exercise the muscles of children, of boys and girls, would they feel the sarcasm if complimented upon the profundity of their intellect? Surely no activity in education that has captured so much of the program, both in time and in courses, ought to proceed without the establishment of a fundamental point of view regarding its place in education.

2 EDUCATIONAL PROGRESS AND HARD TIMES*

By Clifford L. Brownell, Ph.D.
Associate Professor of Physical Education, Teachers College, Columbia University

These are amazing days in education. Affairs are moving so rapidly that no one can say, with assurance, how far they will go or in what ultimate direction.

Within the past eighteen months we have seen forces of rigid economy directed toward education. We have seen educational standards go plunging downward until sometimes only the skeleton of traditional subject matter remains. We have seen programs, introduced within the past decade and heralded by pedagogical leaders as important forces for social betterment, emasculated or scrapped for lack of financial appropriations. We have seen teachers' salaries reduced, or left entirely unpaid; and we have seen scores, indeed hundreds, of teachers dismissed from positions in which efficient service was being given. And, with it all, we have seen the great mass of teachers carrying on, as they have done in past crises, hoping and generally believing that the momentum of educational progress will finally burst through the engulfing fog of hard times—a confidence which may or may not be justified. The situation is common to public schools and to institutions of higher learning.

Nor is this chaotic condition confined alone to education. Its deeper significance is to be found in the basic organization of state, national, and international affairs. Side by side with the accumulation of enormous national wealth and huge production of industrialized commodities, one finds the ghost of mass idleness; the increasing loss of employment due to mechanized industry; a tragically inequitable distribution of wealth— breadlines and crowded theaters, squalid slums and sumptuous estates within a stone's throw of each other; a flagrant disregard for law and order; the admitted failure to apply the scientific method to political problems; and the disappear-

ance of old and cherished loyalties which held men together in faithful allegiances.

The international situation is equally precarious. The current world scene is characterized by competition among industrial countries for raw materials and markets for manufactured products; tariff barriers which isolate thoroughly interdependent nations; and harassed countries practically bankrupt but armed to the teeth and haunted by the fear of aggression.

Rarely, if ever, in the history of civilization have local, state, national, and world affairs been in such a social and economic turmoil. Leaders in historical and political affairs are divided in their opinions as to the outcome. Some contend that the era of peace and plenty is "just around the corner." Others see in the world picture the doom of civilization. Still others observe the germination of a new society with traditional culture finally supplanted by ideals of socialism or communism; or at least a decidedly different civic order than the one to which we are accustomed.

Whatever the outcome, the need for education seems signally apparent. Irrespective of the turn civilization takes, and notwithstanding the state, national, or international ideals which are set up, education must still assume its responsibility as the greatest factor in moulding public opinion and in training youth for the fullest realization of these ideals.

In the light of relative values, is it not strange that those who control our political and financial affairs should apply the pruning knife first to educational budgets? Is it because education is less well organized to fight back than some other municipal and state enterprises? Is it because education may have failed to fulfill the obligation for which it was intended and is, therefore, guilty of "sanctified squander"? Is it because education represents such a long term investment before dividends begin to accumulate that taxpayers fail to recognize its true importance? Probably the

*From The Journal of Health and Physical Education **4**:10-11, 61, April 1933.

answer lies somewhere in the middle ground with contributing factors accumulated from various sources.

What may be still stranger, however, is that school officials commit the same error for which the city fathers are accused. As soon as school budgets are decreased, the appropriation for health and physical education is among those to be dropped entirely or greatly impoverished. Again we might ask the same questions as before. Is it because our program is not well organized and consequently vulnerable to such attacks? Is it because the outcomes of health and physical education are too idealistic, too fanciful, or too obscure for educational authorities to realize its importance?

There is but one way to answer these questions. Either health and physical education has a contribution to make to education or it has not. If there is a place for this program as it is now organized, or as it may be redirected, we should fight for it.

Existing conditions of society are bound to make new and important demands upon education. The school population is increasing in practically every state. Social economists declare that a return of the prosperity era of recent years will not banish the spectre of unemployment. Due to the mechanizing of industry literally hundreds of thousands of men will be free from labor for a greater part of the working day. What is to become of this group? Shorter working hours with commensurate compensation is proposed. Whatever plan is finally adopted, attention *must* be focused upon leisure-time education. If an industrialized civilization results merely in an unoccupied populace, it is doomed unless education can lift the great masses of people to higher levels of achievement through a wise use of this leisure. The right type of education will present a forward step of great magnitude.

Schools of the future must be less concerned with imparting information alone than with the task of creating whole personalities—intellectual, social, physical—who are keenly aware of the changing world about them and of their responsibilities as citizens in it. In the past the burden of teaching the conventional subjects has so completely absorbed the time and energy that little was left for accomplishing the broader ideals of education. Persons who think of retrenchment in terms of returning to the three R's as a means of preparing youth for the new civilization might just as well argue that military implements and tactics

of the Civil War period would be successful now in defending our country against an invading foe. Ideals of culture must be understood in terms of twentieth-century needs, and not defined by concepts that belonged to the liberal education of our forefathers.

Will this new education become a reality? Only time can tell. Some contemporary educational writers assert that each national crisis is followed by an intensified era of progressive education. Perhaps society realizes its failure to produce the type of citizens desired and hastens to make amends. We are reasonably sure, however, that the kind of education that survives the present predicament will represent the economic, political, and social ideals of our citizenry.

In this general picture of the new school, what is to be the rôle of health and physical education? We must begin to revise our plans, restate our policies, re-establish our standards, and determine our objectives in keeping with changed conditions.

It has been charged that health and physical education has sailed the high seas of education blindly, without a compass and with a rather hazy port of destination. On the other hand, one is confronted with irreparable evidence from hundreds of instances where health and physical education has achieved rightfully a position of educational significance in public school or college communities. The time is at hand when we must courageously work together in redirecting our program to serve changed social needs.

In the new education, our program has at least three functions to perform. First, the improvement of physical and mental health. Second, the development of neuro-muscular skills in activities which may be used for leisure-time pursuits. Third, the inculcation of certain desirable social traits, with physical education serving as a laboratory in which approved civic responses are allowed to germinate and then are carefully nurtured. The initial task is to prepare definite and precise objectives which we wish to accomplish. The selection of these objectives, choice of activities, evaluation of outcomes, and plans of organization will depend upon local conditions and problems encountered. *The essential feature is to have a program which is practical and in accord with the educational needs of the community.*

The mental and physical health of youth is important. Unfavorable conditions associated with economic depression have lowered the morale of our fellowmen. Dr. Mayo's statement that every other bed in our hospitals is occupied by a patient placed there because of nervous or mental disorder is appallingly significant. Protection and improvement of personal health is a matter which must receive attention through private, non-official, and public initiative. If education is concerned with the child's entire personality, the school is compelled to assume at least a partial responsibility in protecting his health.

Leisure time, occasioned by fewer hours of labor, makes new demands upon education. While music, art, literature, and the drama are noteworthy, the rôle of physical education is peculiarly significant in the development of skills in activities which may be used to provide hobbies and avocations which supplement the more serious tasks of earning a livelihood. Through the appeal of big-muscle activity, physical education not only prepares for leisure, but provides opportunity for the perpetuation of group loyalties, and other civic traits fundamental to a democratic society. The degree to which these characteristics are nurtured depends upon the effectiveness of our organization.

The leaders in educational thought have, in the past, championed the cause of health and physical education. Their support continues, although the effectiveness of these pronouncements is subdued. Removed from the actual scenes where curtailment is in progress, their wisdom is unheard in the thunder of local turmoil. The task of winning the fight is placed squarely upon us.

Organized opposition to health and physical education exists in numerous cities and states throughout the country. Municipal boards of education and college presidents have reduced budgets, and states have refused appropriations and have attempted to repeal laws. A precedent once established frequently spreads. It is our responsibility to unite definitely against allowing this precedent to assume such proportions that state and local governments will find it convenient and easy to eradicate health and physical education. Budgets may be curtailed in our de-

partment as in others, but so great an educative force as ours must not be destroyed.

School boards and taxpayers think of health and physical education in terms of you and me and our program. Do they know us? Do they know our programs? Lacking the tradition enjoyed by numerous other subjects, we must double our efforts to acquaint them with the aims and purposes of health and physical education.

Have we talked with our people about the effect of the present crisis upon the children of our community, the state, and the nation? Are we making an effort to cultivate a widespread interest in health and physical education in our daily contacts with students and citizens? Education is so important that it should be one of the last municipal or state enterprises to suffer if budgets must be reduced. Roads and bridges can be built tomorrow. Youth lives and learns today.

In conclusion it is essential to point out that whatever achievements result in the perpetuation of health and physical education, they will not be the task of any one man, however wise and efficient, or the work of any committee, however national in scope or distinguished in personnel. They will be made possible only by the genuine outpouring of human friendship, of cooperating one with another, of thoughtful preparation for the tasks to be accomplished, and of generous and sincere devotion to the service of education. Health and physical education is caught in the devastating whirlpool of economic retrenchment and social unrest. Sometimes it is the target of political thrusts gauged to curry favor with an uninformed constituency. Every person who has chosen health and physical education as a profession must rise to the occasion, and, imbued with the determination to move forward rather than backward, meet the opposing forces with all the energy and training he can command. Education leads to civic illumination but this fact alone fails to light the lives of those who are deprived of the opportunity for physical, intellectual, and social regeneration which lies before us.

3 HOW ABOUT SOME MUSCLE?*

By C. H. McCloy
Research Professor of Anthropometry and Physical Education,
State University of Iowa

For a profession that has glorified the physical side of man from before 500 B.C. until, shall we say, A.D. 1915, the physical education literature of today is strangely silent about the more purely body-building type of objectives. From the time of Homer to shortly after the time of Thorndike, the emphasis will be found to have been on the physical education *through* the physical surely, but also education and pure training *of* the physical, for its own sake as well as in Education's sacred name. Then came the leavening influence of Thorndike's psychology and of Dewey's philosophy, enlarging our concepts of how to educate, and as a profession we made real progress. But this progress was made at the expense of the old model. We did not overhaul it, but, following the leadership of Mr. Henry Ford, we traded in all of the old equipment on the new. Twenty-five centuries of good experience—as all who read history discerningly must agree—abandoned over-night in favor of a new equipage whose worth to the ultimate consumer, the child, was yet to be appraised!

And why? Your guess is as good as mine. I think it was possibly a combination of three things. First, many physical educators had an inferiority complex. A few sensitive souls still have. We didn't quite belong to the educational fraternity; we were just "physical directors." The new educational emphasis gave us "face," and, exulting in our new importance, we forgot most of the fundamentals; we didn't want to be "strong."

Second, it was so easy to "educate" with a game book and a whistle. It saved time, preparation, and the mastering of a lot of difficult skills and the techniques of progression.

The third possibility is that the leaders of the new educational movement, carried away by enthusiasm for this valuable addition to our armamentarium, overstressed the new—as Luther

Gulick was wont to do in pioneering a movement—and gave the impression to their pupils and to the readers of their papers and books that the educational aspect of physical education was *all* that really mattered. Whatever the reason, the result has been that when physical education went to college and added psychology, character education, mental hygiene, tests and measurements, and the new organization of principles to the curriculum, it quietly dumped most of its body-building emphasis into the educational garbage can and set it out on the curb.

Has this been justified? Let us examine the evidence. Ignoring the varsity teams who, we shall grant, get enough muscle building, let us consider the average pupil. I doubt if more than one-fifth of our physical education classes in the schools of today get enough exercise to contribute materially to any significant organic stimulation. Widespread strength testing has shown that in whole cities there are scarcely 20 per cent of the pupils who have a normal amount of strength, measuring strength by Rogers' Physical Fitness Index, and Rogers' norms for strength are quite moderate in their demands.

But is more muscle desirable? Let us marshal a few of the arguments.

1. In 1907 J. M. Tyler published *Growth and Education,* a book which was and is a milestone in physical education. In the first few chapters were assembled a galaxy of biological facts which have never been seriously disputed. Tyler showed that vigorous exercise of the great fundamental trunk and limb muscle is utterly essential during youth and young adulthood for the purpose of stimulating the normal growth and development, not only of the fundamental organ systems of the body, but of the brain and mind as well. And this exercise need—an inheritance from the remote past—a need for more than pretty movements. What is needed is a great deal of oxidation within the body tissue. Tyler made clear the fact that an organism whose evolu-

*From The Journal of Health and Physical Education 7:302-303, 355, May 1936.

tionary development was dependent upon vast amounts of exercise could not function adequately on a semi-sedentary ration of activities.

2. The psychological literature of late years has spoken much of the fact of body-mind unity, but this same literature has usually gone on thinking and writing as though the school child was all mind. We in physical education, with our growing over-emphasis upon the educational aspect of physical education, are apt to fall into the same error. *Our organism is more body than mind,* and it is only through the adequate functioning of all of it that the most desirable functioning of even the brain occurs.

3. From the standpoint of mental hygiene, a number of studies in our own field, some of them unpublished, have shown that the physically undeveloped child and adult tend to develop inferiority feelings which grossly affect his social responses and his character and personality development. We need adequate bodies as well as play and recreation. While this is only a part of our mental hygiene problem, the physical educator should not forget that it is an important part and one which can be corrected fundamentally only by developing an adequate body. It cannot be eradicated simply by *understanding* the problem. "Facing reality" in this case means developing the muscles, attaining a better carriage, and in general developing and educating the *physical* self.

4. In considering the significance of physical strength, let us develop an imaginary situation. Let us suppose that some one were to request you to wear, day and night, a well-fitting canvas jacket lined with lead shot which increased your weight 25 per cent. Your response would undoubtedly be something like the following: "Don't be absurd! Why to burden myself with a load like that would result in my being utterly fatigued by early afternoon. I should have no energy for constructive work, and at night I should be too tired even for recreation. The added strain upon my heart would be harmful, and I would be so constantly fatigued, particularly during the latter part of the day, as to render myself more susceptible to minor infections, such as colds." And you would be right. However, the man who is 25 per cent overweight is constantly subject to just this strain. The same difficulty is encountered by an individual of a given normal weight who has only four-fifths of the normal amount of muscle. From the standpoint of fatigue, of inefficiency of movement, of susceptibility to minor infections, he

finds himself in the same situation as the individual who is 25 per cent overweight; and this individual, be he school child or adult, does suffer some of the following handicaps.

a) Fatigue, both acute and chronic. — The undermuscled person tires easily. (Rogers has well shown that a certain type of endurance is almost perfectly correlated with strength relative to weight.) But this person is not only susceptible to occasional acute fatigue; this fatigue piles up in a normal life of activity. At the end of each week he finds himself almost sick — intoxicated with the accumulated poisons of a fatigued organism.

b) Muscular inefficiency. — Studies in the physiology of muscular work demonstrate that the efficiency of muscular contraction depends upon there being an optimum load on the muscle. Thus a muscle that is overloaded has a smaller work efficiency than one which is not loaded too heavily. The person of less than normal strength, in addition to his constant fatigue, is working always at a relatively lower level of efficiency than would have been the case had his strength been up to normal for his weight.

c) Susceptibility to infections. — It is the common experience of many people that their susceptibility to colds and like minor infections is greatest when they are most fatigued. This, for some reason, seems to be more true of continuous chronic fatigue than of moderate acute fatigue. Possibly it is because in almost all acute fatigue the person has recovered before the process of infection has proceeded far enough to be dangerous. It is a common observation that more colds result from mingling in crowds at the end of a week than under similar circumstances at the beginning of the week, when an individual is more rested. The under-muscled person is much more constantly in a condition in which he is susceptible to such infections than is the stronger person. This, of course, has nothing to do with specific immunities which seem to be dependent upon a chemical condition within the body.

d) Functioning of organic systems. — Tyler also established the fact that an abundance of muscular exercise strengthens the day-by-day functioning of all of the organic systems. This is perhaps most easily understood in the relationship to the functioning of the heart. This organ, which is itself a muscle, is exercised and developed by being forced to exercise more strenuously in response to the vigorous exercise of the voluntary musculature. The individual whose muscular experience is constantly at a subnormal level has a heart that is as flabby as his arms and legs. In times of emergency, not so much the running for a street car as the fighting of pneumonia, the weaker heart is more apt to be unequal to the task than is the well developed heart. Adequate strength is good life insurance.

All of these facts seem to me to afford convincing evidence that we need better-developed muscular systems than the current literature in our profession is demanding. The argument frequently proposed by non-physical-education educators that since we are not all going to be truck drivers we do not need to be well developed is not, it seems to me, even intelligent. A young adult having to toss his body, weighing from 100 to 200 pounds, around an office, up and down stairs, or around a golf course, needs a normal musculature. Therefore, I should like to propose that as a profession we re-think the whole problem of our more purely *physical* objectives, and that we emphasize them more. I yield to no one in our profession in my belief in the educational importance of physical education when adequately organized and taught; the health education procedures are also of great importance. But the basis of all physical education—developmental, educational, corrective, or any other aspect of our field—is *the adequate training and development of the body itself*—that should be thought of as a fundamental prerequisite.

In recent years there has been a swing towards an emphasis upon adult education. The physical educator, on the whole, has not kept up with this movement. Anyone who takes the trouble to visit city turnvereins, or some of the business men's classes of Y.M.C.A.'s, and sees young sixty-year-old men playing fast volleyball or doing stunts on the apparatus with ease and grace and enjoyment—stunts that the majority of physical education teachers of today cannot do—or who sees fifty- and sixty-year-old Englishmen playing soccer or cricket or rowing, almost with the vigor and finish of youth, must realize that most middle and old age deterioration is a function of inactivity. Adults who forget to maintain that muscular development which is the prerequisite to a youthful old age pay the penalty by losing that youth; it is hard to lose one's youth and gain it back again, but it is relatively easy to keep it.

It seems to me that the time has come when we may be expected to retain more than one major objective at a time in our intellects—to keep hold of the good of the past while we add from the worth-while contributions of today. May we suggest that the best defense is a strong offense; and for the physical educator who feels inferior to someone who scorns the physical as he glorifies the Great American Intellect, it is suggested that he espouse the cause of body-mind integrated unity, fortify himself with the facts, and merrily conduct a major offensive that will place the feeling of inferiority back where it belongs, upon the physically feeble mental advocate who is simply compensating with much talk for his own feeling of physical inadequacy.

How about some muscle?

4 THE CULTURAL DEFINITION OF PHYSICAL EDUCATION*

By Rosalind Cassidy**

The long view of history shows the fascinating truth that beliefs and values within a given society, held in relation to man and his body, have resulted in quite different concepts and programs in what we today call Physical Education. I have long held that in any given period, Physical Education is culturally determined by what man thinks of his body, how he thinks of himself in relation to his body, and how he thinks his body should be trained, exercised, disciplined, developed, educated; in effect how he, himself, should be trained, exercised, disciplined, developed, educated. This is true whether in a society where the self and the body are believed to be separated or in one where there is an acceptance of the scientific research which shows man as a moving, thinking, feeling, expressing, unified organism.

This relativity concept is clearly seen in historical perspective when the belief about man and his destiny are contrasted in the education and Physical Education programs in Sparta with the quite different programs in Athens in its "Golden Age." Again in the Middle Ages, man's concept of himself and his body and how his body should be educated provides a startling contrast with those held during the Renaissance. In our day, Hitler's Third Reich set forth fanatical concepts of

man's relation to the State, which gave all of education and Physical Education that truly terrible definition.

In our own society from Puritan times, from the conquest of the Western frontier on to today's interworld frontier, a whole new definition of man's needs and values is being described. The changes in education and in Physical Education in the United States from the early settlements to the present can only be understood and interpreted accurately if seen as results of the beliefs held about the human individual, his nature, needs and purposes.

We are now in a period of exploding new knowledge and unprecedented speed of change, which demand answers for today and directions for tomorrow. So the central question is, as we are rushing toward the 21st century, "What are the concepts, the values and the forces now shaping and continuing to re-shape our definition and our programs, and thus forcing us to identify a new physical education for a new and different world?"

The human organism: An area of fact, which must be examined as we study this question, has to do with the almost overwhelming onrush of new knowledge about the human organism-functioning-in-our-particular-society. This day of space exploration is centering a tremendous amount of research on the staying powers of the human organism in environments other than that of our little earth-world, bringing new understandings of man's functioning both on earth and in space.

We have known, even though we quite often do not act upon this fact, that the organism is by its very nature unified. This unity is manifest not only in psychosomatic functioning, but also in the interrelationships and interactions with the organism's environments. These concepts have given us the term sociopsychosomatic even though unfortunately we, quite often, do not apply this reality in our current programs. Certainly they are

*From Quest **4:**11-15, April 1965.
**About the Author:* Dr. Rosalind Cassidy, the most prolific woman author in the profession, has long been known for her pioneering ideas, the quality of her thinking and the breadth and depth of her leadership, in and out of the profession, and, in this and other countries. Beginning with her first book, *The New Physical Education,* which she co-authored with Thomas D. Wood, M.D., she has been at the frontier edges of the pioneering efforts in physical education. *Quest* is fortunate in presenting this, her latest article. A Gulick Award winner, a former president of The American Academy of Physical Education, Dr. Cassidy has been and is being recognized for the eminent roles she has played on the American educational scene.

abrogated when we continue to separate the individual into physical, mental and social packages.

A study of the most recent facts concerning the individual's growth and development within our society gives a new and convincing understanding of the central role of movement in the development of the human organism. These facts give a whole new realization and conviction about the role of movement in human life. Movement is indeed central in relating, in learning, in self-acceptance, in establishing self-values, in becoming. There is a built-in thrust for health or self-actualization. We know that authoritarian treatment brings fear which in turn brings hostility and alienation from others. We know the relation of personal involvement to responsibility, to individual purpose. We increasingly realize the urgency of responsible co-operative behavior in our society. We are continually gaining new concepts and understandings showing the relation of perception to behavior, to purpose and to personal meanings.

There are whole areas of fact around the need for extending purposes, for widening perceptions, for encouraging individuality and creativity as means of relieving fears and tensions in uncertain and threatening times.

The normal individual is born with the power to move. It is through effective movement that he experiences and expresses, learns, develops his human potentialities. Is human movement then the primary concern of what we now call Physical Education?

Individual and society: Now what current societal facts should be identified as a base for a rational answer to the central question: How is Physical Education being redefined today?

If the culture determines the definition, what are some of the areas of cultural change that we must understand and relate to our own field? My search for fact was made in three areas: first, technology and automation, providing more leisure; second, world tension, exploration of outer space, development of atomic power, stress in living, rapidity of change; third, threats to democracy both at home and abroad.

Our technical development is creating more leisure. There is already a four-day work week for many people and there is less vigorous activity on the job. How are we to make this leisure re-creative?

We are truly in a strange new time. John Dille in the September 25th, 1964 issue of *Life* Magazine in an article entitled "The Revolution Isn't Coming—It is Already Here," says:

It will probably come as a surprise to those Americans who think the matter is still up for debate, but the Space Age is here. The most daring, revolutionary, and expensive step in mankind's long effort to master his environment is not off in the dim future. It is not even just over the horizon. It is with us—now.

We are living in an anxiety culture with political and social conflict at home, with world tensions and conflict and with the unknown threat or promise of other worlds yet to be explored. The speed of change, the fears and wonders of outer space, fears caused by the atomic threat, economic and political uncertainties, threats from Cuba and the USSR, the unknown world influence of the rising new nations of Asia and Africa, and the great looming peoples of Red China from whom probably the greatest threat will come, and at home the great Civil Rights revolution of our time—all are aspects of our anxiety culture. These result in threats to individual significance, to individual security, and create a need for greater self-awareness, for a deeper self-knowledge through a movement literacy and a movement vocabulary, for knowing how to spend energy according to one's tempo and biochemical make-up and ways to find relief from tension and strain. Today there is need for self-knowledge related to how to achieve and maintain one's own fitness for living with these realities.

The threats to democracy at home and abroad have been made dramatically clear. What with the events in Cuba, and Vietnam, in Mississippi, in Alabama, the Freedom March and the race riots in our immediate experience, we have the continuing problem of the ideological conflicts between democracy and fascist concepts. Today the valuing of each person regardless of race, color or creed is our most urgent national problem, and thus becomes a primary concern for all areas of education. An area of fact related to this is that enhancing the self is an essential to valuing one's own self, which in turn is central to valuing others. Today the individual needs respect for and encouragement of individuality, self-responsibility, and skills in problem-solving on the basis of fact versus half-fact or propaganda.

A new definition: These central facts of our day, relating to the individual in our United States society, show clearly the need for a new definition and a clarification of our discipline. First, as we look at what we know about the human individual in his growth and development aspects, we know we are using inaccurate terminology. There is no separate physical nor mental. We do not have History Education nor English Education as a disciplinary field. We can neither think clearly nor can we communicate convincingly because we are not using accurate terms. When we talk of Physical Education, we have neither described an essential educational discipline nor a body of knowledge. What is Physical Education in our country today? Is it gymnastics, drill, tests, games, sports, dance? We are not ourselves clear as to purpose or content and therefore we cannot make our field clear to others. Ever since the educational soul searching after Sputnik, Physical Education in many places has been termed "non-mental" or "non-academic" and has been curtailed. This will continue until we make the definition for our day and time from the facts, beliefs and values of our contemporary society.

New dimensions: This discussion has attempted to do just that. It seems clear that for our day we must see our area as human movement, scientifically based and expressive in outcome. *The Art and Science of Human Movement* is the cultural definition being made for Physical Education by societal forces today. In our studies at UCLA we have been saying that our discipline is "all the facts, knowledges and understandings of human movement related to the fullest actualization of the individual within his social setting." Physical Education is no longer a useful term. Its use actually confuses us and our publics. By many, Physical Education is equated with intercollegiate athletics or exercise systems. But when human movement is seen and made manifest as our discipline, it will be accepted as closely related to other expressive areas. When we say human movement we mean all of human movement, the whole range of human movement from the toddling baby to the art form. We must understand the sciences of man but we must be closely organized with the expressive arts of

which human movement, non-verbal and expressive, is an integral part. When this view is generally accepted by our profession, dance, for instance, could not possibly be organized as a separate department—even the performance aspect, any more than painting, sculpture, ceramics, at the exhibition level, can be separated from the whole discipline of art.

The greatest challenge, drawn from these facts about human individuals in today's society, then, is to describe, accept, develop and incorporate in curriculum patterns our Body of Knowledge. This will involve capacity and willingness to study in depth, our unique contributions; it means that we have to be able to change and to forego vested interests and discard inaccurate terminology; we will have to be creative in teaching and research, and we will have to see our discipline as concerned with the whole range of human movement.

The disciplinary approach: Declaring for this concept of our Body of Knowledge and using accurate terminology will help each one of us to wider and clearer perceptions of our discipline. And having such new dimensions, we then will be able to communicate more clearly and convincingly with both students and colleagues. A new view will show us and our colleagues the necessity of much needed interdisciplinary research to rid ourselves of restricting outmoded terminology and a narrow concept of our field and its contribution to human development. It will free us to move with the changes of this fabulous new day, and to contribute fully to the enrichment of human life. This is our new dimension. It truly is *our greatest challenge* and *our grave responsibility.*

Note: Parts of this article were included in a presentation made at the opening session of the Western Society of Physical Education for College Women, Tucson, Arizona, November 8, 1962, and are included in their 38th Annual Report.

SUPPLEMENTAL READINGS
1930-1939

5. Berry, Charles Scott: A broader concept of physical education, The Journal of Health and Physical Education **3**:3-4, September 1932.

6. Francis, R. J.: Toward a philosophy of physical education, The Journal of Health and Physical Education **10**:216-217, 258-259, April 1939.

7. Kirk, H. H.: A superintendent looks at physical education, The Journal of

Health and Physical Education **9:**538-540, 585-586, November 1938.

8. Neilson, N. P.: The value of physical education and health in the school program, The Journal of Health and Physical Education **4:**21, April 1933.

9. Tighe, B. C.: Physical education in its functional aspects, The Journal of Health and Physical Education **6:**14-15, 51, December 1935.

10. Trilling, Blanche M.: The significance of physical education in modern life, The Journal of Health and Physical Education **9:**3-5, 57-58, January 1938.

11. Wayman, Agnes R.: Trends and tendencies in physical education, The Journal of Health and Physical Education **4:** 16-18, 62, February 1933.

1940-1949

12. Bookwalter, Karl W.: Why physical education? The Physical Educator **1:** 41-43, October 1940.

1950-1959

13. Dodson, Taylor: The fourth dimension, The Physical Educator **12:**66-67, May 1955.

14. McCloy, C. H.: A planned physical exercise program? or "What would you like to do today?" The Physical Educator **10:**38-41, May 1953.

15. McCloy, C. H.: A reply to Dr. Williams and to Dr. Oberteuffer, The Physical Educator **10:**101-103, December 1953.

16. Metheny, Eleanor: The third dimension in physical education, The Journal of the American Association for Health, Physical Education, and Recreation **25:** 27-28, March 1954.

17. Oberteuffer, Delbert: In response to C. H. McCloy, The Physical Educator **10:**72, October 1953.

18. Streit, W. K., and McNeely, Simon A.: A platform for physical education, The Journal of the American Association for Health, Physical Education, and Recreation **21:**136-137, 186-187, March 1950.

19. Ulrich, Celeste: A fairy tale (which turned out to be a parable), The Physical Educator **15:**100-101, October 1958.

20. Williams, Jesse Feiring: A reply to Dr. McCloy, The Physical Educator **10:**71, October 1953.

1960-1969

21. Brackenbury, Robert L.: Physical education, an intellectual emphasis? Quest **1:**3-6, December 1963.

22. Duncan, Ray O.: Quo vadis? Journal of Health, Physical Education, and Recreation **37:**22, January 1966.

23. Wagner, Ann: A basic concept of physical education, The Physical Educator **21:**169-170, December 1964.

1970-1979

24. Annarino, Anthony A.: The five traditional objectives of physical education, Journal of Health, Physical Education, and Recreation **41:**24-25, June 1970.

25. Clumpner, Roy A.: Convincing the public of basic values is the key, The Journal of Physical Education and Recreation **49:**22, 65, September 1978.

26. Struna, Nancy: Teaching movement—our common goal, The Journal of Physical Education and Recreation **48:**12, June 1977.

27. Triplett, M. Evelyn: Physical education's principal emphasis is upon building a fit America, Journal of Health, Physical Education, and Recreation **41:** 30, 44-45, June 1970.

ASSIGNMENTS
Individual activities

1. Discuss *education through the physical* as it relates to the objectives of physical education.
   ARTICLES: 1, 2, 5-10, 12, 13, 17, 18, 20, 21, 24, 25, 27.

2. Compare the opinions of physical educators from different decades relative to *education through the physical*.
   ARTICLES: 1, 2, 5-10, 12, 13, 17, 18, 20, 21, 24, 25, 27.

3. Discuss *education of the physical* as it

relates to the objectives of physical education.
ARTICLES: 3, 14, 15, 22.

4. Compare and contrast *education through the physical* and *education of the physical*.
ARTICLES: 1, 2, 3, 5-10, 12-15, 17, 18, 20-22, 23, 24, 25, 27.

5. Discuss the *human movement* approach to physical education.
ARTICLES: 4, 16, 23, 26.

6. Compare and contrast the *human movement* approach with *education through the physical* and *education of the physical*.
ARTICLES: 1-4, 5-18, 20-27.

7. Compare modern societal conditions with those of earlier decades and indicate their influence on the objectives of physical education.
ARTICLES: 1-4, 5, 6, 8-11, 27.

8. Indicate the implications of article 19 for modern physical education programs.

Group presentations

1. Panel discussion
   a. TOPIC: *Objectives and contributions of physical education.*
   b. PARTICIPANTS: Physical educators representing various decades and various points of view.
   c. FUNCTIONS: To present, explain, and defend the positions taken by the selected authors.
   d. OBJECTIVES OF PRESENTATION: (1) To identify specific authors and time periods and (2) to clarify the *education through the physical,* the *education of the physical,* and the *human movement* approaches to the objectives of physical education.
   e. ARTICLES: 1-4, 5-18, 20-27.

2. Drama
   a. TOPIC: *Societal trends and their impact on physical education.*
   b. PARTICIPANTS: Physical educators representing various decades.
   c. FUNCTIONS: To enact a meeting of past and present authors in which they discuss societal trends and their impact on the objectives of physical education.
   d. OBJECTIVES OF PRESENTATION: (1) To identify specific authors and the time periods during which they lived, (2) to indicate relevant societal trends of the various time periods, (3) to indicate contributions of physical education to an industrialized society, (4) to emphasize similarities between modern society and societies of earlier years, and (5) to indicate societal trends and needs that have led to the modern concept of physical education.
   e. ARTICLES: 1-4, 5, 6, 8-11, 27.

"Therefore as I said before, our children from their earliest years must take part in all the more lawful forms of play, for if they are not surrounded with such an atmosphere, they can never grow up to be well conducted and virtuous citizens."

Socrates, 420 BC

CHAPTER TWO

Elementary school physical education

When did you last observe young children totally immersed in the pure exhilaration of physical activity? Their boundless joy and unabashed enthusiasm for movement are inspirational! They love to move, to explore space, to test their limitations, which they occasionally appear to be convinced are nonexistent! The joy of the physical experience registers on their faces as they are prompted to run ever faster, climb ever higher, accomplish ever more difficult feats of skill. These children are truly teachable—ready, willing, and able to learn.

What better time than the elementary years to introduce children to the experiences and knowledge that will provide the foundation for future development and enjoyment? Where could we find a more receptive audience? These children are eager to learn the physical skills that will enable them to meet new and greater challenges. They can hardly wait to jump as high, throw as far, run as fast as the "big kids," and they are willing to work diligently in pursuit of these goals.

MEETING THE NEEDS

How should physical educators attempt to meet the needs of these elementary school youngsters? What approach should be taken in assuring them opportunities for challenge and progress? Is recess, free play, or an occasional game of dodge ball sufficient to sustain and nurture their aspirations for success in the physical realm? Although some controversy exists within the profession about the specific approach that is appropriate for elementary school physical education, there appears to be consensus that organized elementary school physical education programs are essential for building a strong foundation for future skill and personal development. Physical educators tend to agree that just as math students must learn that $1 + 1 = 2$ before they attempt to master complicated equations, so must students of physical activity understand the basic fundamentals of movement before they attempt to master the complex movement patterns that hold the promise of even greater joy and pleasure. Just as the foundation for subsequent acquisition of intellectual accomplishment must be laid during the formative years, so must the foundation for subsequent acquisition of physical prowess be laid during those years. The purposes are clear, but the processes through which the objectives may be realized are frequently the subject of disagreement and debate.

Currently, the most popular approach to elementary school physical education is referred to as the *human movement* approach. This concept of physical education is inseparable from the discussion of the objectives of physical education as presented in Chapter 1. Proponents of the human movement approach contend that the objectives of physical education relate directly to movement and that a study of movement itself at the elementary school level is the most reasonable route toward the development of efficient and effective movement skills. This basic premise on which the human movement approach is founded appears to present few, if any, problems. Questions arise, however, in attempting to arrive at a single definition of the human movement approach. Confusion also exists with respect to definitions of many of the terms and techniques inherent in the approach. An investigation of the literature reveals that many authors have devised their own definitions. Although many of these definitions may be similar, there are variances in connotation sufficient to create a degree of disturbance among those who wish to study and understand this approach. For these reasons, a brief introduction to the most fundamental concepts of the human movement approach is provided.

The term used most frequently in conjunction with the human movement approach to physical education is *movement education*. Carol DeMaria's definition serves as a basic explanation of movement education:

Fundamentally, movement education is a problem-solving approach to developing efficient and effective motor development in children through their understanding of the basic principles of body motion.*

There are three basic techniques through which the goals of movement education may be realized. These techniques are movement exploration, problem solving, and guided discovery. Patricia Tanner and Kate Barrett define these terms as follows:

Movement exploration: Movement exploration implies a process where the most open or freest environment is allowed for learning to take place. This is the situation where the learner is not given a specific series of directions for operation nor tied down to any particular outcome. The intent in this process is to give students the greatest opportunity for self-discovery in and on their own terms.

Problem solving: With a literal translation of problem-solving, it is obvious that the term implies an environment within which the child must come to grips with the process of solving problems, where he becomes better able to differentiate between solutions that are applicable or appropriate to the problem and those that are not. This interpretation of the method called problem-solving means that children are no longer dealing with movement solely on their own terms but are being influenced to varying degrees by the structure of the task. All possible solutions are not necessarily known to the teacher in this strategy.

---

*DeMaria, Carol R.: Movement education; an overview, The Physical Educator **29**:73, May 1972.

Young children enjoy movement experiences.

Guided discovery: Guided discovery is best described as being a particular strategy within the wide range of problem-solving. Guided discovery is the strategy where the outcome or solution to the problem is known to the teacher but is not necessarily initially known by the learner. The role that the teacher plays is to guide the child by question or clue through exploration of a variety of possible solutions to a desired outcome, or certain desired outcomes.*

Basically, then, the movement education approach to physical education involves the development of efficient and effective movement. This development is achieved through the application of specific techniques to the study of movement itself rather than through the traditional approaches involving structured, organized game activities and command teaching. Further study will demonstrate the fact that games may be included as a portion of movement education, but they serve to incorporate the results of the process rather than constitute the process itself.

Advocates of movement education suggest many advantages and benefits for this approach to elementary school physical education. The following list of its values represents the viewpoints of several authors. The proposed values are listed in random order, and the listing does not reflect any priorities with respect to their merits. According to these authors, movement education contributes to: (1) the development of body management skills; (2) the development of interest and involvement in movement; (3) the provision of opportunities for success; (4) the development of physical fitness; (5) the elimination of discipline problems; (6) the development of an awareness of the body in movement; (7) an understanding of the part played by movement in daily life; (8) the development of self-discipline and self-direction; (9) the provision of opportunities for creativity and self-expression; (10) the development of skills that can be adapted to game and dance situations; (11) the provision of opportunities for satisfaction and fun; and (12) physical, mental, emotional, and social development.

These suggested values are impressive, but they are not persuasive to all physical educators. Some feel that physical educators may be "going overboard" for movement education. Some of the objections voiced by some professionals are that: (1) movement education may be only a fad; (2) students need to learn the correct execution of skills rather than to explore all of the possibilities; (3) development of creativity is not guaranteed; (4) experimentation may result in injury or in the development of bad habits; (5) development of self-direction is not guaranteed; (6) teachers may try to take the easy way out; (7) students may develop one-sided programs; and (8) many teachers are ineffective using this approach.

Arguments on both sides of the issue appear to have merit. Prospective physical educators should be aware of the variety of viewpoints within the profession

*Tanner, Patricia, and Barrett, Kate: Movement education; what does it mean? The Journal of Physical Education and Recreation **46:**20, April 1975.

Children using movement skills in a game situation.

and should have some knowledge of the arguments surrounding this approach to physical education.

This discussion does not provide an all-encompassing explanation of the human movement approach to elementary school physical education. The intention is to introduce this aspect of the profession and some of the ideas proposed by physical education scholars. The advice of Marion Broer serves as a valuable guide to this aspect of professional preparation in physical education:

Does it really matter if some physical educators wish to use the term "movement education" instead of physical education? Will we go on dissipating our efforts in disagreement over such questions until the profession comes clattering down about our heads like a deck of cards? Or will we recognize that there are many avenues leading to the mansion which is this profession, and that there are many blocks and columns which support its framework? Instead of attempting to close possible access roads, will we help to widen them? And rather than working to crumble some of the blocks and columns, can we reinforce all with the steel of cooperative study and bind them together with the mortar of shared hypotheses and conclusions to build a solid foundation from which the profession can, in the future, rise to new heights? This is our challenge.*

---

*Broer, Marion R.: Movement education; wherein the disagreement? Quest **2:**23-24, April 1964.

WHO SHALL TEACH?

Once the purposes of elementary school physical education have been identified, attention must be directed to their implementation. Some of the obvious questions are: Who should be responsible for teaching elementary school children movement fundamentals? Should elementary school physical education be taught by the regular classroom teacher, or should this instruction be the responsibility of a specialist, the professional physical educator?

The ramifications of these questions are far reaching, and the ultimate solution to the problems they pose depend on the answers to additional questions: Does the teaching of elementary school physical education require knowledge and expertise in excess of the training and qualifications of an elementary school classroom teacher? Are enthusiasm for movement and a love of children sufficient to qualify an individual as a physical educator at the elementary school level? Is it possible for an individual preparing to teach elementary school to prepare simultaneously to teach physical education? On what considerations should the final determination of responsibility for teaching physical education at the elementary school level be based?

Although current professional opinion tends to support the contention that elementary school physical education should be taught by a professionally prepared physical educator, prospective physical educators should be aware of the historical aspects of the controversy. In May 1931, Marguerite Behrensmeyer and Kathleen Skalley Davis published opposing viewpoints in *The Journal of Health and Physical Education.** Several decades intervened, and elementary school physical education programs underwent major alterations; however, the issue was still being discussed as recently as 1972 when Hanson explored the topic in an article published in *Quest.*† During the intervening years, the pros and cons of the classroom teacher versus the physical education specialist were debated at length. Authors addressed themselves primarily to the following three options: (1) the classroom teacher as the sole instructor of physical education, (2) the physical education specialist as the sole instructor of physical education, and (3) the physical education specialist and the classroom teacher working cooperatively in an effort to maximize the benefits of the physical education program. The synopsis of these articles in Table 1 reveals that most of the attention was directed toward the capabilities or lack of capabilities of the classroom teacher rather than toward the positive attributes of the physical education specialist.

Further investigation of the literature reveals additional suggestions that are worthy of consideration. Hanson introduces an alternative approach as she pre-

---

*Behrensmeyer, Marguerite: Who shall teach physical education in the elementary schools? The special teacher, The Journal of Health and Physical Education, 2:28, 59-60, May 1931; Davis, Kathleen Skalley: Who shall teach physical education in the elementary schools? The classroom teacher, The Journal of Health and Physical Education, 2:29, 53-54, May 1931.

†Hanson, Margie R.: Professional preparation of the elementary school physical education teacher, Quest **18**:98-106, June 1972.

Table 1

The classroom teacher may:

1. Accord physical education less attention than other subjects.
2. Direct greater emphasis toward those areas in which standardized measurement may be used.
3. Not have had the appropriate professional preparation.
4. Need intervals of relaxation away from the children.
5. Be able to choose the most beneficial time period.
6. Be familiar with the individual physical, mental, and social differences of the students.
7. Have more opportunities for generalization.
8. Be able to choose units of work to be studied.
9. Correlate physical education with other subjects.
10. Be aware of the kinds of activities needed.
11. Encourage wholesome relationships among children, teachers, parents, and the school.
12. Improve the health of the children, the school and playground organization, the interpretation of democracy, the interrelationship between physical education and other subjects, and safety practices.
13. Adjust the time allotment for physical education to the overall program.
14. Lack sufficient training in physical education.
15. Already have extremely heavy professional demands.
16. Recognize the need for elementary school physical education.

The physical education specialist may:

1. Possess skill in guiding the teaching of the elementary school child.
2. Possess knowledge of the characteristics and interests of elementary school children.
3. Understand children's total learnings through visits to the classroom.
4. Possess a knowledge of child growth and development.
5. Have been a physical education major.

Cooperation between classroom teacher and specialist may:

1. Furnish valuable assistance to the classroom teacher.
2. Provide a better total curriculum.
3. Provide a better interpretation of physical education as a portion of the total curriculum.
4. Provide for more economical use of resources.
5. Enhance the physical education teacher's status.
6. Eliminate the argument over which is best.

sents a solution that may be achieved through professional preparation.* She explores the possibility that since all teachers need to understand the total school program, perhaps the dual major in elementary education and elementary physical education could produce educators who are prepared to function effectively in both the classroom and the gymnasium. This solution appears to eliminate the controversy over which individual is better prepared to teach elementary school physical education, but it raises additional questions. What about the time and energy required of a student who pursues both an elementary education major and an elementary physical education major? Will the elementary education major ultimately be expected to attain degrees in other special subjects, such as music and art? What are the ramifications of Hanson's suggestion?

Obviously, the responsibility for elementary school physical education in-

---

*Ibid.

struction must be taken seriously. The literature provides many viewpoints from which the solution may be derived. The one constant is the fact that the youngsters in the elementary schools deserve the very best instruction available. Every professional decision should be based on that underlying premise and should be defended in that light.

SPREADING THE WORD

The importance of elementary school physical education programs is generally recognized and supported by the physical education profession. Among physical educators, there appears to be no controversy over the desirability of such programs. However, the general public frequently is unaware or unconvinced of the necessity for regular, planned physical education programs at the elementary school level. Did your elementary school offer a physical education program? If so, did this program comprise planned, structured learning experiences, or was it primarily a free-play period? Did the secondary school physical education program that you experienced complement the elementary school program through planned, sequential activities based on previous acquisition of skills and knowledge? If your elementary school physical education program was inadequate or, possibly, nonexistent, can you suggest reasons for this? If we *know* that elementary school physical education is worthwhile and necessary, why aren't these programs as deeply entrenched in some of our school systems as other subjects are?

Are physical educators partially to blame for this apparent lack of understanding? Have we failed to convince the public of the values and benefits of elementary school physical education? Worse yet, have we failed to develop basic beliefs about the importance of elementary school physical education? Do you, as a prospective physical educator, believe that physical education should be included in the elementary school curriculum? More important, do you know *why* you believe as you do? If we, as professional physical educators, cannot articulate sound reasons for our belief in elementary school physical education, how can we expect to convince those individuals who possess the authority to institute these programs in the schools? The people with the authority are the taxpayers and the members of the boards of education. They decide the amounts of monies to be allocated to the schools and the programs into which these funds are to be channeled. Many of these individuals did not receive instruction in physical education at the elementary school level; therefore, their frames of reference might lead them to believe that such programs are unnecessary. How are we to convince them that physical education is a beneficial, justifiable, necessary component of the elementary school curriculum? We must be able to present solid evidence that our convictions are based on fact, not fancy.

Physical education literature reflects strong arguments supporting the need for elementary school physical education programs:

    1. The elementary school age is the best time for children to learn good body mechanics.

Appreciation for physical education begins in childhood.

2. The elementary school age provides teachable moments for skills.
3. Elementary-age children are less self-conscious, less fearful, and less inhibited.
4. Children need activity for proper growth and development.
5. Young children are willing and eager for activity.
6. Through activity, children may establish a basis for wholesome development.
7. Emotional problems, postural defects, unacceptable social habits, and poor attitudes may be recognized early.
8. The young child needs opportunities for the release of excess emotion.
9. The young child may learn patience, group consciousness, courage, and self-control through physical education activities.
10. Physical education could contribute to the development of a favorable

self-image, creative expression, motor skill, physical fitness, and knowledge and understanding of human movement.

11. Physical education may influence the degree of success the child experiences in work and play.
12. Physical education provides an important avenue for nonverbal communication.
13. Physical education provides an opportunity for the child to develop into a fully functioning individual.
14. Through sensorimotor experiences, the child learns how to learn and how to relate socially to others.

Challenges are often spontaneous and irresistible.

15. Mental development may be enhanced through physical education activities.
16. Elementary school–age children have the capacity to develop high degrees of neuromuscular skill and tend to learn these skills at a faster rate than do older children.

Not every physical educator can be expected to accept each of these arguments. It does appear, however, that most of them are quite persuasive and should serve to convince the most adamant "doubting Thomas" that the elementary school physical education program is a necessity rather than a frill.

As a prospective physical educator, your task is not completed simply by memorizing a list of the arguments supporting elementary school physical education programs. In reality, your mission as a professional will be fourfold: (1) to determine and understand the purposes and objectives of physical education at the elementary school level; (2) to study and learn as much as possible about physical education and elementary-age children so that you can defend elementary school physical education on a scientifically formulated and philosophically sound basis; (3) to take advantage of every opportunity to convince the public of the need for elementary school physical education programs; and (4) to make certain that the elementary school physical education programs under your leadership are of a quality sufficient for children in your classes to recognize and appreciate the values of physical education. If these future taxpayers and members of boards of education find physical education to be a rewarding, worthwhile experience, they should be kindly disposed toward the contributions of physical education when they become adults. Consequently, through your efforts, future generations of youngsters may be assured opportunities for experiences that promise them life-long challenge, accomplishment, and enjoyment.

SUMMARY

The literature on elementary school physical education reflects three primary areas of concern: (1) the selection of the most appropriate approach to the teaching of physical education at the elementary school level, (2) the designation of the teacher who should be responsible for the elementary school physical education program, and (3) the formulation of a sound base of knowledge that will serve as the foundation for the justification of physical education as a vital component of the elementary school curriculum.

These areas of concern are not independent units of consideration but interrelated and interdependent issues. Solutions to each issue will depend, in part, on solutions to the others. It would be impossible to lend intelligent support to a particular approach to elementary school physical education before determining justification for the inclusion of physical education in the elementary school curriculum. Likewise, it would be difficult to establish convictions about the designation of physical education teaching responsibility before determining the purposes of physical education and the approach that should be taken to achieve them. An equally difficult task would be to attempt justifying the inclusion of physical education in the elementary school curriculum before determining the objectives of physical education and the most appropriate approach toward their realization. Each area of concern hinges on the others, and definitive solutions to the problems each poses will require an understanding of the ramifications of all its aspects.

1 SOME THOUGHTS FOR MOVEMENT EDUCATORS*

By H. Joe Blankenbaker and Myron W. Davis**

The movement education approach to teaching elementary physical education has created considerable excitement among elementary teachers and physical educators. As is often the case with new ideas in physical education, the bandwagon effect is very much in evidence in the literature and at professional meetings. Many teacher preparation colleges now offer entire courses devoted to movement education for the future elementary classroom and physical education teachers. In addition, there are numerous workshops and in-service training sessions offered throughout the country in order to familiarize teachers with movement education concepts. This interest created by movement education has brought new pressures calling for physical education programs in all elementary schools. The concern for elementary physical education created by movement education has inspired many elementary school administrators to re-evaluate their present physical education programs in relation to the children's needs.

REASONS FOR THE POPULARITY OF MOVEMENT EDUCATION

Movement education is very much in line with current thinking in education. It is a conceptual approach to learning that has as its foundation an understanding of various movement elements. Movement educators encourage students to use

their intellectual abilities and to translate them into psychomotor activities. Movement education is an individualized approach to learning, thus keeping with educators' concern for individualization of instruction. Because movement education is an individualized approach, there is little concern for the grade level of the children. Instead children work within their own capabilities and at their own rate of speed with little concern for measuring up to specified standards.

A major selling point for movement education is that it is success oriented. The children solve movement problems designed so that they can respond in a manner that is within their own range of ability and experience. No solution is incorrect so no child fails. Therefore, the negative attitudes so often developed toward physical education by many young students are avoided. Concentrated activities in sports and games and much of the accompanying competition have been eliminated. Such activities were usually dominated by the superior athletes and were a source of embarrassment to the lesser skilled. Movement educators are concerned with developing fundamental skills and an understanding of movement that can later be utilized in such games and sports.

Another strong selling point for movement education is the encouragement of creativity. Traditional physical education tends to stifle creativity by forcing all children to do the same thing at the same time. Movement education actually encourages creativity by challenging students to find different ways to solve problems in move-

*From The Physical Educator **32:**28-30, March 1975.
**Drs. Blankenbaker and Davis are both on the faculty at Georgia Southern University.

ment. Teachers of movement education do no demonstrating of the proper techniques nor do they encourage imitation of others. Children are left to explore many possible combinations and sequences of movement while the teacher acts primarily as a guide. In fact, most movement education advocates feel that skill in movement is not at all required of a successful teacher.

Perhaps the greatest appeal of movement education is the fact that it represents a break with the traditional type of program. Many educators believed that such programs were meeting the needs of only a select few of the students. Such programs were too often headed by aspiring coaches who presented their students with scaled down secondary programs. Movement education offers an attractive alternative to such situations.

SOME CONSIDERATIONS FOR MOVEMENT EDUCATORS

Despite the popularity of movement education, several physical education leaders have expressed reservations about this approach. One such reservation concerns the advisability of completely abandoning the so-called traditional physical education program consisting of games, rhythms and self-testing activities in favor of a program structured completely of movement education. Locke (6) pointed out that the traditional program may not be as lacking in merit as some movement education advocates have claimed. He states that failures attributed to traditional elementary physical education are not the result of methodology but a failure of teachers and teacher preparation programs.

Kirchner (5) also commented on the use of certain aspects of the traditional program along with a movement education program. He stated that "movement education is but one integral part of the physical education program, not its replacement." Kirchner suggested that the movement education approach should be especially emphasized in the areas of rhythms and self-testing activities, but basic instruction in games and sport skills may sometimes require a different approach.

One of the features of movement education is the problem-solving technique used to create learning situations. The movement problems are presented to the children in such a manner that there is seldom one single correct solution. Because one child's solution is just as correct as another, all members of the class are assured

of experiencing success. However, a problem arises when a child solves problems in a manner which violates certain principles of movement—i.e. in learning to propel objects by throwing them, one child consistently throws with the wrong foot forward. This child is solving the problem, but in doing so is reinforcing a bad habit. Dauer (2) pointed out that concern for quality movement includes occasional suggestions by the teacher about necessary adjustments in movement patterns so that learning proceeds properly. In this case the movement educator could perhaps counter with a problem involving throwing with the left foot forward. Most physical educators would agree that the early years are very important in the development of proper movement habits. It is therefore essential that students not be left completely to a trial and error method of discovery in the essentials of movement.

Humphrey (3) also cautioned against elementary programs structured completely around movement experiences and skill learning. He states that "the fallacy of this approach is that the child does not have sufficient opportunity to make practical application of these experiences." In other words games and activities requiring the use of skills learned through movement education should be a part of the elementary program. Children could then use their increased understanding of movement qualities in situations other than those created by posing movement problems. In such games and activities, the learning that can take place should be emphasized and the competition involved should be de-emphasized. Another possible weakness of programs involving only movement experiences and general skill learning is alluded to by both Kirchner (5) and Locke (6). They pointed out that research in motor learning contradicts the contention of movement educators that movement education can develop a general capacity for movement. Locke stated that transfer of learning skills takes place when skills practiced closely resemble the ultimate skill to be learned.

A final caution concerns the teacher of movement education. It is not true that it is easy to teach movement education. In fact a sound movement education program should involve more planning and teacher involvement than the traditional program. It takes considerable planning in order to present movement problems to the children so that each solution is related to the next problem. The movement problems must not be just a number of isolated trial and error attempts at unrelated problems. Instead, each activity that the teacher offers should be compatible with the objectives of the problem. This cannot be accomplished without considerable teacher planning.

The considerations discussed here are not meant to discourage teachers from using movement education. Instead, they are presented as an attempt to convince teachers to first acquire a thorough understanding of the objectives and methodologies of movement education before using this approach. Teachers should realize that changing to a complete movement education program will not assure them of having a meaningful and worthwhile program. Teachers should also realize that movement education may not always be the best approach to meeting the needs of the student. It is the responsibility of the teacher to select the approach which will best meet the objectives of each particular class period. Teachers should not allow the current popularity of movement education to alter their approach to physical education without first considering the merits as well as the limitations of movement education.

REFERENCES

1. Dauer, Victor. *Essential Movement Experiences for Preschool and Primary Children.* Minneapolis: Burgess Publishing Company, 1972, p. 49-62, 102-118.
2. Dauer, Victor. *Dynamic Physical Education for Elementary School Children.* Minneapolis: Burgess Publishing Company, 1971, p. 52-56.
3. Humphrey, James H. *Child Learning Through Elementary School Physical Education.* Dubuque, Iowa: Wm. C. Brown, 1974, p. 51.
4. Kirchner, Glenn et. al. *Introduction to Movement Education,* Dubuque, Iowa: Wm. C. Brown, 1970, p. 9-11.
5. Kirchner, Glenn. *Physical Education for Elementary School Children.* Dubuque, Iowa: Wm. C. Brown, 1974, p. 536-545.
6. Locke, Lawrence. "A Critique of Movement Education," in Sweeney, R. T. *Selected Reading in Movement Education.* Reading, Massachusetts: Addison-Wesley Publishing Company, 1970, p. 187-199.

2 TOWARD AN UNDERSTANDING OF BASIC MOVEMENT EDUCATION IN THE ELEMENTARY SCHOOLS*

By Elizabeth A. Ludwig
Professor of Physical Education at University of Wisconsin, Milwaukee.
This article was prepared at the request of the Physical Education Division Editorial Committee.

Many early efforts to stimulate and support a "foundations" approach to content in physical education are only now taking a firm hold in the elementary school programs. Confusion still exists at this time in this country as to the meaning and status of "basic movement education," "movement fundamentals in physical education," "movement exploration," and other terms used to designate a specific program or content in physical education. In historical perspective neither the confusion nor the experimentation with the program content is new.

A review of changes related to philosophy and programs in physical education in the United States since the first quarter of the century reflects shifting emphases from rigidly structured programs of gymnastics, calisthenics, folk dance, and simple games stressing physical fitness to carry-over activities that develop recreational and social values through participation. With the changes in general educational philosophy that occurred since the era of Dewey, a number of forward-looking leaders in physical education

*From Journal of Health, Physical Education, and Recreation **39**:26-28, 77, March 1968.

were re-thinking the philosophy of physical education slowly but surely as early as the 1920's. Pioneers such as Thomas D. Wood, Jesse F. Williams, Rosalind Cassidy, and Dorothy LaSalle were pointing to "new directions in physical education." Clue words such as "child-centered," "the whole child," "opportunities for creative expression," and "skill learning" appeared in the professional literature in physical education in the 1920's and 1930's.

From the early 1930's on a number of movements or changing directions were taking form although their relevance to contemporary changes are only now becoming evident. Margaret H'Doubler proposed new concepts in educational dance and applied her theories to basic movement education as the foundation for all physical education. Women's physical education staffs in a number of universities and colleges introduced courses in "movement fundamentals." More functional approaches to the study of kinesiology and biomechanics and research in motor learning were begun at the universities of Wisconsin, California, Iowa, Illinois, Nebraska, and others. The fields of physical therapy, mental health, and recreation contributed to an understanding of the importance of motor skill development in the healthy and well-adjusted individual. Research findings from many areas of the child growth and development field affirmed the developmental needs of the child and the wholeness or integrity of the individual; studies in learning, motivation, and other aspects of educational psychology suggested more effective teaching procedures. The growing responsibility of the school in meeting the child's basic needs in the area of motor skill development as well as in the more academically-oriented areas was recognized.

During this time the leaders in physical education who were vitally concerned with the content of the elementary school physical education program as well as the improvement of teaching on this level included Gladys Andrews, Delia Hussey, Edwina Jones, Dorothy La Salle, Ruth Murray, Elsa Schneider, and others.[1] It is important to mention this vanguard of leaders because the present effort to improve the elementary school physical education program has, in turn,

been stimulated by individuals who were influenced by the efforts of these early leaders.

After World War II there was a great deal of travel between this country and England, Germany, Scandinavia, and other European countries. Ideas were exchanged, and a fresh look was taken at developments at home and abroad. Changes were occurring all over the world, and in England there developed a different approach to basic movement education in elementary schools. English teachers were seeking answers to the same problems that had interested teachers in the United States for many years. Leadership in England was centered in the Ministry of Education under the influence of such persons as Ruth Foster, Peter Stone, and Diana Jordan. They found support in Rudolph Laban, an Austrian dancer who came to England during the war and introduced his theory of movement principles. Two Anglo-American workshops and a number of visits helped develop a strong rapport and unity of spirit among English educators and their American counterparts. Some of the materials and procedures developed in England were instituted in this country by those who participated in the workshops and study trips.

Certain periods in history seem right for the flowering of ideas which may have been generating for a long time. During the past ten years there has been a concerted rush for better programs of physical education in the elementary schools—better teaching procedures, better facilities, and better prepared teachers. During this decade there has also been a renewed effort to include in the elementary school program a greater emphasis on basic movement experiences as the foundation for all physical education, particularly in the primary grades.

SUPPORT FROM OTHER AREAS OF RESEARCH

A related emphasis in American education that has given support and impetus to these efforts is the interest in creativity in teaching and the recognition of the importance of developing and encouraging the creative learner. A great deal of research has been undertaken in this area in an effort to identify the factors that are important in producing both the creative teacher and the creative learner. Providing the opportunity for the learner to solve his own problems or to discover unique solutions to problems in which he is given certain basic conditions and factors to work with is considered necessary in "best learning." This

---

[1]The writer recognizes that our indebtedness extends to many other men and women who have exerted leadership both on the local and national levels. This list is not meant to be inclusive.

ability is one of the characteristics of the creative thinker and performer. Experimentation with approaches to teaching consistent with the newer theories of education that stress problem solving and discovery on the part of the child has been a part of the attempt to develop the total basic movement education approach. The importance of discovering common elements in fundamental motor skills and of analyzing activities for their use in basic movement patterns also has been recognized as essential. Accelerated research in kinesiology, motor learning, teaching theory, and other related fields has given support to interest in developing programs that include more than the traditionally structured games, dances, and gymnastics of the typical elementary school program.

The following brief summary of "where we are" at this time in the development of basic movement education programs is made with full recognition of the fact that there are no two programs exactly alike, nor should there be, if the tradition of the American educational philosophy is to be maintained. Generally speaking, however, certain elements of philosophy are recognized and certain common content and teaching procedures are used.

It is generally agreed that basic movement education is the foundation upon which all the activity areas of physical education are built. It is also agreed that the aim of basic movement education is to help children become aware of their own potentials for moving effectively in all aspects of living, including motor tasks involved in daily activities for work or recreation. Fundamentals of movement are explored and built upon so that a child develops an awareness of each part of the body as it moves through space, with variations in time and force. A child learns to use his body with power and economy of movement; he experiences in a wide variety of ways the degree of effort required for easy, fluent, and efficient performance of the particular movement task he has undertaken. He solves problems dealing with gravity, direction, and controlling objects such as balls as conscious experiences. Efficient and effective movement results within the innate capacity of each child.

Some children will learn to perform better than others because they have inherited this kind of facility. Some individuals will become more highly skilled than others because they work harder and/or have the desire to perform well. Each individual is limited, however, only by his inherited potential.

EXPERIENCES IN BOTH BREADTH AND DEPTH

The *content* of the program consists of all those experiences that will assist the child to develop skill in using his body—stretching, twisting, rolling, jumping, hanging, running, walking, hopping, sliding, pushing, pulling, throwing, catching, striking, and the many combinations of these movements that are within the capability of the human structure. It is not possible here to categorize these movements or to discuss those which are basic and which are combined movements. Movement patterns are developed in anticipation of later use in games, skills, dance, gymnastics, and other activities. The content is not chosen randomly; it has a purpose and is planned but it is not necessarily specific to a particular game or other structured activity. The child experiments with many variations of movement or skill so that his experiences are in breadth as well as depth.

The content of a particular lesson may deal with problems that emphasize the concept of space and the body's relationship to space or may place emphasis on the factors of time and force. Because these are interrelated, all are always considered, but one may be stressed for a particular reason. Obstacles or restricting equipment may be used to give the child experience in handling his body within certain limitations. The use of restricting equipment is fundamental to providing for the many experiences needed as a basis for developing games and gymnastics skills. Balls, paddles, ropes, hoops, bean bags, and stilts and climbing, hanging, jumping, and vaulting equipment may be used. When emphasis is placed on developing an understanding of the quality of movement, the effect of rhythm and timing, tone and design, a foundation for the more structured aspects of dance is fostered. Emphasis on timing and rhythm also aid in the highly developed skills of the expert gymnast and diver.

The *process* or the teaching procedure used is a direct outcome of the content in that the movement experiences are those of the child and he must learn for himself what his body can do. Problem solving is involved, the problem of learning to handle the body. Sometimes the problem proposed by the teacher involves pure exploration by the child. Then the solution will be largely discovery. Some problems may be restricted in order to elicit specific responses. The teacher uses the particular technique suited to the needs of the child and the task. Basically, problem solving and the move toward discovery are intimately related to the content.

An aspect of both content and method that is stressed is teaching the "why" and "how." Principles of movement mechanics, rhythm, and timing plus other knowledges and understandings are taught. This procedure is not unique to basic movement education but the fundamental purposes of this method are consistent with and require the total involvement of the child—both intellectually and physically. The challenge of this kind of involvement gives the physical education experience an exciting dimension that tests children of every range of ability and gives purpose and meaning to the program.

The values that are evident to those who have been working with children using basic movement education as a medium of instruction may be summarized as a conclusion to understanding basic movement education in the elementary schools.

1. Success is within the reach of every child because the goals are personal. Quality performance (at different levels) is stressed, expected, and usually obtained from the children.

2. Self-discipline and self-direction are expected results. The child must make decisions constantly and he is held responsible for them.

3. The situation provides a laboratory for freedom to create, to express, and to try out one's own solutions without fear of being a loser or a "dub."

4. When game elements are added, an "it" or a "goal," the child is ready for the challenge because he has attained a comfortable degree of skill.

5. Although children are quite serious and totally involved in the teaching-learning situation, satisfaction and fun result. This is movement with a purpose and is so recognized by the child; it is exciting to him, as skills develop and success is experienced.

3 TEACHING PHYSICAL EDUCATION IN THE ELEMENTARY SCHOOL— WHOSE RESPONSIBILITY?*

By James H. Humphrey

In the course of discussing responsibilities for teaching physical education in the elementary school one might explore the responsibilities of parents, board of education members, administrators, teacher-training institutions, teachers, and even the pupils themselves.

Where should the responsibility for providing desirable physical education learning experiences for elementary school children be placed? Certainly, this is not a question which can be dealt with in a single pat answer. Indeed, there does not appear to be "a one best plan" of teaching

that fits all possible conditions. For instance, if you are one who believes that the classroom teacher cannot do a satisfactory job in this regard, you could be referred to various school systems throughout the country where classroom teachers have been teaching physical education for many years with gratifying results.

On the contrary, those of you who hold tenaciously to the idea that the special teacher of physical education should be confined to the secondary school level, could likewise be referred to school systems which have used special teachers of physical education in the elementary school for a good many years with a great degree of success.

*From The Physical Educator **18**:104-106, October 1961.

It is a well known fact that many postulations have been made with respect to the place of the classroom teacher and the physical education teacher regarding which of these individuals is in the best position to provide desirable physical education learning experiences for elementary school children. It is also well known that some individuals are "dyed-in-the-wool" proponents of either the use of the classroom teacher or the special teacher in absolute form. It is also well known that various arguments can be set forth which purport to show how one plan is more advantageous than the other.

Let us examine some of the present ways of designating responsibility for teaching physical education in the elementary school. After studying this problem for a number of years and after surveying scores of school systems in order to determine the current status and trends in this area, we have found that it would be suitable to arrange these plans or ways of designating teaching responsibility into about five major classifications as follows:

1. The classroom teacher having the responsibility in all grades, 1 through 6 with some sort of supervisory or consultant service. About 27 per cent of the cases fall in this classification.
2. The classroom teacher and special teacher both responsible and working together in one way or another. The range of time that the classroom teacher and special teacher are actually on the scene at the same time ranges from one day per week to daily. About 26 per cent appear to use this plan.
3. The classroom teacher having the responsibility for Grades 1-2-3 with assistance, and the special teacher responsible for Grades 4-5-6. There are about 19 per cent in this classification.
4. The special teacher having the responsibility in all grades 1 through 6. About 12 per cent may be included in this classification.
5. The classroom teacher having the responsibility with no assistance whatsoever. There are about 7 per cent in this classification. It may be recalled that a recent study[1] conducted by the Office of Education showed 15 per cent in this classification. One might speculate that the difference is due to the fact that in the Office of Education study, 15 per cent of the school systems did not employ physical education specialists in any way. Whereas, the results reported here are from school systems which employ either a director or supervisor who is in charge of the physical education program for the system.

[1] Schneider, Elsa, "Ten Questions on Physical Education in Elementary Schools," U. S. Department of Health, Education, and Welfare, Office of Education, Washington, D. C. 1957.

There are a variety of more or less "unclassifiable" plans and about 9 per cent are found to be in this classification. In these plans both the classroom teacher and the special teacher share the responsibility in one way or another.

First, the plan where the classroom teacher has the major responsibility for all grades with some sort of resistance. The trend here appears to be overwhelmingly in the direction of retention of this plan. Also it is noted that almost 40 per cent of the people reporting see a trend toward greater cooperation of the classroom teacher and the person providing the assistance for the classroom teacher. There are various factors influencing the trend to retain this particular plan. Among others these factors include:

1. The general philosophy of elementary education is in terms of the so-called self-contained classroom.
2. Lack of funds—This could be interpreted to mean that they would use special teachers if they had the money to employ them.
3. Better program of inservice education.
4. In about 20 per cent of the cases it was indicated that better undergraduate preparation of classroom teachers influenced the trend to retain this plan.

The next plan was the one that involved the classroom teacher and the special teacher working and teaching together in one way or another. One noteworthy trend reported in over 90 per cent of the cases indicates that there is more and more cooperation between the classroom teacher and the special teacher. The major factors influencing this trend are a changing philosophy of elementary education, and better program of inservice education.

The third plan, that of having the classroom teacher assume the responsibility for Grades 1-2-3 with assistance and the special teacher responsible for Grades 4-5-6 also is characterized by some interesting trends. One of these is that it is becoming more common to have the classroom teacher assume the entire responsibility for the primary level while the special teacher spends practically all his time with Grades 4-5-6. As might be expected the most prominent factor influencing this trend is a better program of inservice education.

In the *fourth plan,* that of having the special teacher responsible for the teaching in all grades 1 through 6, there is a decided trend to continue with this procedure. The major factors suggested as influencing this trend are: lack of interest of the classroom teacher, poor teaching on the part of the classroom teacher, and insufficient preparation of the classroom teacher. It is extremely important to mention here that while the special teacher has the responsibility for practically all direct teaching under this plan, it was reported that the classroom teacher may play an important part by assisting the special teacher in such ways as: informing him about the traits and characteristics of children, by interpreting objectives, philosophy and certain problems of the elementary school, and assisting with problems of control and discipline.

Where the classroom teacher is responsible for teaching without any type of assistance at all, the trend seems to be in the direction of retaining this *plan*. However, this does not mean that this is entirely satisfactory because the main reason for the trend is due to lack of funds. In other words, in all probability if funds were available some sort of assistance might be provided for the classroom teacher.

A detailed analysis of these various ways of designating teaching responsibility reveals that in approximately 88 per cent of the cases the classroom teacher shares the direct teaching responsibility. And, in the remaining 12 per cent, while the classroom teacher does not share in direct teaching, she at least has some sort of indirect responsibility. One trend which was in evidence in all of the plans where the classroom teacher and special teacher were involved was that there appears to be more and more cooperation between the classroom teacher and the specialist in this particular endeavor.

In view of the fact that both the classroom teacher and the special teacher are so mutually involved it is strongly recommended that more effort be directed toward developing the cooperative role of the special teacher and the classroom teacher rather than attempting to justify one plan as having a certain degree of merit over the other.

The special teacher and classroom teacher need to pool and share their knowledge and abilities so that the most desirable learning experiences may be provided for children through physical education. Each has a great deal to contribute and should be encouraged to do so. This idea precludes a type of philosophy that is based on the premise that the special teacher exists *only* for the purpose of giving the classroom teacher a "break" or a rest when the specialist appears on the scene. It is questionable

that there is any more validity in this idea than in one that would purport to have an arithmetic specialist teach arithmetic for the purpose of giving the classroom teacher a respite from arithmetic class.

The preceding statements should not be interpreted to mean that the classroom teacher should not have some rest and relaxation during the trials and tribulations of the school day. Indeed, the school day should be organized so that the teacher has some free time to herself. However, it is very questionable whether that time should *always* be taken from the one area in the elementary school curriculum where the teacher can perhaps learn more about her children than from any other school experience. It does not seem too unreasonable to assume that most *good* classroom teachers will want to take advantage of observing their children in that best of all laboratories of human relations—physical education.

If the special teacher and classroom teacher are to benefit from each other's experiences, the classroom teacher should be present whenever the special teacher teaches the class. There are exceptions to this of course because there are times when it may be most desirable for the special teacher to work alone with the children.

When the classroom teacher and special teacher work together the special teacher should not be expected to assume *all* of the responsibility for direct teaching. On the contrary, the specialist should have opportunities to observe the classroom teacher conduct the class so that constructive suggestions may be offered for consideration. This practice is particularly important because the classroom teacher can then benefit from the suggestions of the specialist and make application of the suggestions when she handles the class alone.

The special teacher and classroom teacher should know what to expect from each other. This means that it becomes the responsibility of the special teacher to "learn the language" of elementary education. For example, if the classroom teacher is working on a particular social studies unit, she should feel free to call upon the special teacher to suggest physical education learning activities that will help to develop the concepts and large understandings involved in the unit. Similarly, the special teacher should have in his repertory of activities those which contain inherent concepts in arithmetic, science, language arts and the other curriculum areas. In this way the special teacher is able to show the classroom teacher how physical education can be used as a most desirable learning medium in the development of concepts and understandings in the other areas of the elementary school curriculum.

In order for the special teacher to provide such learning activities it is essential that he have a full understanding of the subject-matter areas of the elementary school curriculum. At the same time the classroom teacher should attempt to develop and improve upon those competencies which are most useful in helping her to provide desirable physical education learning experiences for the children in her class.

In summary, a few general considerations should be taken into account. The specific way of designating the responsibility for physical education learning experiences will depend upon a number of factors. Among others these include: (1) the underlying philosophy of the local group; (2) interest, preparation, and experience of personnel; (3) time allotment and facilities; and (4) funds available for implementation of the program.

In the final analysis the plan of teaching employed must be compatible with the local situation and, above all, one that most satisfactorily meets the needs of all of the children. For this reason it seems essential that all factors pertinent to local conditions be thoroughly appraised and evaluated before a definite plan of action is taken. Moreover, any plan that is established should be subjected to continuous evaluation so that desirable practices may be retained or modified and undesirable practices eliminated as the occasion demands.

4   SELECTED RESEARCH FINDINGS WITH IMPLICATIONS FOR ELEMENTARY SCHOOL PHYSICAL EDUCATION*

By Richard T. Trimble**

A review of the professional literature reveals a limited amount of research relating to program concepts in elementary school physical education. Therefore, in addition to his own field, the elementary school physical educator must examine research findings in related fields such as sociology, psychology, social psychology, and physiology, if he desires to obtain available information relative to program improvement.

Research findings supporting pre-school and elementary school education naturally have considerable application for physical education in the elementary school. The importance of early motor learning experiences to optimize the po-

tential for later learning has been reported rather extensively in the literature. Of particular significance have been the observations of Jean Piaget and G. N. Getman. A summarization of their findings indicates that early motor experiences are very important in establishing a child's understanding in relation to people, objects and concepts. In effect, the child learns how to learn and how to relate socially to others through sensori-motor experiences. It is quite obvious, then, that it is not desirable to leave such experiences to chance occurrence. An intelligently planned physical education program can be instrumental in systematically providing these needed experiences.

Another researcher, Benjamin Bloom, authored a book entitled *Stability and Change in Human Characteristics* which has implications for early childhood and elementary school physical education. In this book, Bloom stated that fifty per-

*From The Physical Educator **29**:123-124, October 1972.
**Dr. Trimble is an administrative assistant in the Graduate Department of Physical Education, College of Physical Education, University of Illinois, Champaign.

cent of adult mental capacity has been acquired by the time a child is 4 years of age and eighty percent of adult mental capacity is acquired by the time a child has reached 12 years of age. Bloom also indicated that changes in mental capacity are greatest during the period when a child is undergoing rapid growth.

The implication of Bloom's findings for elementary school physical education relates to the fact that physical education is a highly motivating activity for most children. Therefore, it seems logical to utilize this motivational effect of physical education not solely to promote physiological improvements, but also to promote psychological and sociological gains as well. This application could promote more cognitive learning than is typically acquired in traditional physical education programs. Some obvious methods that facilitate cognitive learning are problem solving, exploration, and the integration of physical education activities with other areas of the elementary school curriculum. The potential and need for improving existing physical education programs to maximize cognitive development is far too extensive a subject to be covered here.

The final research finding to be cited concerns work done by Paul Hunsicker, a researcher in physical education at the University of Michigan. On the basis of his research, Hunsicker has stated, "Most children 10 years of age, have the neuromuscular potential to master the skills required in practically any physical education course currently offered at the college level."[1] In fact, the investigator indicates the rate of learning is actually faster at younger ages. Hunsicker's statements do not imply that an elementary school age person would necessarily have the ability to pass the college level course since size and/or strength may be a limiting factor.

The implications of Hunsicker's findings for elementary school physical education are at least twofold. Certainly indicated is the need to provide neuromuscular activities that truly challenge the child. This evidence also substantiates the viewpoint that planned activity sequences throughout

the child's school life are needed. It is readily observable that many physical educators do not have curricular guidelines that provide knowledge revealing what their students have done previously, what is to be done currently, and what is to be done in the future. This type of planning is essential if a long-term goal is to be achieved in a systematized manner.

These limited remarks certainly do not fully reflect the profound implications of research findings on elementary school physical education. It is the responsibility of the physical educator to become familiar with the available research so that intelligent application of the findings can be utilized to improve elementary physical education programs.

In summary

1. The physical educator in the elementary school must go to other disciplines in addition to his own to become familiar with research findings that have implications for improving physical education programs.

2. Sensorimotor experiences are important in the development of children. The value of these experiences may be enhanced if they are provided systematically and in an intelligent manner.

3. The pre-school and elementary school years of a child's life have great potential for cognitive development. Physical educators must be aware of this potential. Methodology should be utilized which fosters an environment facilitating cognitive learning as well as learning in the affective domain.

4. The neuromuscular capabilities of elementary school age children are often underestimated by teachers. Teachers must not underestimate these abilities or the potentialities of their students will not be reached.

BIBLIOGRAPHY

Bloom, B. *Stability and Change in Human Characteristics,* New York: Wiley and Sons, 1964.
Getman, G. N. *How to Develop Your Child's Intelligence,* Luverne, Minnesota: Announcers Press, 1962.
Hunsicker, P. *What Research Says to the Teacher,* #26 Physical Fitness, Association of Classroom Teachers of the National Education Association, 1963.
Piaget, J. *The Construction of Reality in the Child.* New York: Basic Books, Inc., 1954.

---

[1]Paul Hunsicker, *What Research Says to the Teacher,* #26 Physical Fitness, Association of Classroom Teachers of the National Education Association, 1963, p. 24.

SUPPLEMENTAL READINGS
1930-1939

5. Behrensmeyer, Marguerite: Who shall teach physical education in the elementary schools? The special teacher, The Journal of Health and Physical Education 2:28, 59-60, May 1931.
6. Davis, Kathleen Skalley: Who shall teach physical education in the elementary schools? The classroom teacher, The Journal of Health and Physical Education, 2:29, 53-54, May 1931.
7. O'Keefe, Pattric Ruth: Classroom teachers in physical education, The Journal of Health and Physical Education 10:530-532, 553, November 1939.

1940-1949

8. Curtiss, Mary Louise, and Curtiss, Adelaide B.: The classroom teacher's dilemma, The Journal of Health and Physical Education 17:335, 381-382, June 1946.
9. Manley, Helen: The plight of elementary school physical education, The Journal of Health and Physical Education 19:335, 376-377, May 1948.

1950-1959

10. Champlin, Ellis H.: Let's take first things first, The Journal 21:20, November 1950.
11. Donnelly, Alice: Let's ask the classroom teacher, Journal of Health, Physical Education, and Recreation 29:43, 80, November 1958.
12. Saurborn, Jeanette: Who shall teach elementary school physical education? The Journal of the American Association for Health, Physical Education, and Recreation 21:76, 114, February 1950.

1960-1969

13. Broer, Marion R.: Movement education; wherein the disagreement? Quest 2:19-24, April 1964.
14. Howard, Shirley: The movement education approach to teaching in English elementary schools, Journal of Health, Physical Education, and Recreation 38:31-33, January 1967.
15. Locke, Lawrence F.: The movement movement, Journal of Health, Physical Education, and Recreation 37:26-27, 73, January 1966.
16. Ludwig, Elizabeth A.: Basic movement education in England, Journal of Health, Physical Education, and Recreation 32:18-19, December 1961.

1970-1979

17. Baumgarten, Sam, and others: In defense of movement education, The Journal of Physical Education and Recreation 48:46-47, February 1977.
18. DeMaria, Carol R.: Movement education; an overview, The Physical Educator 29:73-76, May 1972.
19. Elementary School Physical Education Commission: Essentials of a quality elementary school physical education program; a position paper, Journal of Health, Physical Education, and Recreation 42:42-46, April 1971.
20. Hanson, Margie R.: Professional preparation of the elementary school physical education teacher, Quest 18:98-106, June 1972.
21. Jewett, Ann E.: "Would you believe" public schools 1975; physical education for the real world, Journal of Health, Physical Education, and Recreation 42:41-44, March 1971.
22. Ryser, Otto: Are we guilty of malpractice? The Journal of Physical Education and Recreation 47:28-29, September 1976.
23. Tanner, Patricia, and Barrett, Kate: Movement education; what does it mean? The Journal of Physical Education and Recreation 46:19-20, April 1975.

ASSIGNMENTS
Individual activities

1. Discuss the controversy surrounding the movement education approach to physi-

cal education and identify several arguments reflecting each side of the issue.
ARTICLES: 1, 2, 13, 14, 17, 22.

2. Submit a paper either supporting or opposing the movement education approach to physical education.
ARTICLES: 1, 2, 13, 14, 17, 22.

3. Submit a paper examining the various options available in the *who shall teach* controversy.
ARTICLES: 3, 5-12, 20.

4. Submit a documented list of arguments supporting the inclusion of physical education in the elementary school curriculum.
ARTICLES: 4, 9, 10, 19.

Group presentations

1. Panel discussion
   a. TOPIC: *Movement education.*
   b. PARTICIPANTS: Selected movement educators.
   c. FUNCTIONS: To reflect the positions held by various authors in the field.
   d. OBJECTIVES OF PRESENTATION: (1) To identify specific authors and points of view, (2) to explain the concept of the movement education approach to physical education, and (3) to entertain questions relative to the topic.
   e. ARTICLES: 1, 2, 13-18, 21-23.

2. Debate
   a. TOPIC: *Movement education*
   b. PARTICIPANTS: Two teams of three or four students each.
   c. FUNCTIONS: To present arguments for and against the movement education approach to physical education.
   d. OBJECTIVES OF PRESENTATION: (1) To identify specific authors and points of view, (2) to present arguments supporting both sides of the issue, and (3) to convince the class members of the validity of the arguments; class members may vote at the conclusion of the debate.

e. ARTICLES: 1, 2, 13-18, 21-23.

3. Debate
   a. TOPIC: *Who shall teach?*
   b. PARTICIPANTS: Two teams of three or four students each.
   c. FUNCTIONS: To present arguments supporting either the classroom teacher or the special teacher as the individual who should be responsible for physical education instruction.
   d. OBJECTIVES OF PRESENTATION: (1) To identify specific authors and time periods, (2) to emphasize the fact that the controversy has raged for years, and (3) to convince the class members of the validity of the arguments; the class members may vote at the conclusion of the debate.
   e. ARTICLES: 3, 5-12, 20.

4. Drama
   a. TOPIC: *Spreading the word.*
   b. PARTICIPANTS: Physical educators from various time periods; members of a contemporary board of education.
   c. FUNCTIONS: The physical educators are charged with presenting arguments that will convince the board members of the need for elementary school physical education; several of the board members are definitely opposed to such programs; other are undecided.
   d. OBJECTIVES OF PRESENTATION: (1) To identify specific authors and time periods, (2) to present documented evidence of the values of elementary school physical education, (3) to play the roles of devil's advocates who oppose elementary school physical education, and (4) to emphasize the consistency of the positions held by physical educators through the years.
   e. ARTICLES: 4, 9, 10, 19.

CHAPTER THREE

Coeducation in secondary school physical education

"**Then, fresh and blooming, you will spend your time in the gymnasium.**"

Aristophanes, 400 BC

Physical education programs at the junior and senior high school levels present situations somewhat different from those observed at the elementary school level. Generally, most of the problems discussed in Chapter 2 have been resolved and have given ground to other considerations. The controversy of whether the classroom teacher or the specialist should teach physical education has lost its significance. In the majority of secondary schools, one or more physical education specialists are responsible for the program. The task of convincing the public of the need for physical education is not as difficult at the secondary level because of the long-established practice of including physical education in the secondary school curriculum. Methodology is an area of continued interest; however, there is no clear-cut controversy such as the movement education approach versus the traditional approach that exists at the elementary level. Teaching styles vary widely among secondary school physical educators, and the quest to discover the most effective styles continues to keep the profession dynamic.

One of the most significant current trends in secondary schools is coeducational physical education. Because this development is somewhat controversial and because it is addressed more frequently than other issues in professional literature, this chapter is limited to a discussion of the reasons that coeducational physical education has become a reality and of the impact that this trend has had on teachers, students, and programs.

A discussion of coeducational physical education, however, would be incomplete without referring to additional aspects of secondary education, such as curricular revision, discipline, professional cooperation, and humanism in the gymnasium. These topics have a direct relationship with coeducation and are interwoven with the total pattern of secondary school physical education to the extent that separation of the issues is virtually impossible. Therefore, an integrated approach to secondary school physical education with an emphasis on the coeducational aspect should serve as a basis for the development of a better understanding of the current scene.

LEGISLATION: TITLE IX

Title IX of the Education Amendments Act of 1972 specifies numerous regulations for educational institutions that receive federal financial assistance. The stipulation most directly related to secondary school physical education programs states:

A [federal aid] recipient shall not provide any course or otherwise carry out any of its education program or activity separately on the basis of sex, or require or refuse participation therein by any of its students on such basis, including health, physical education, industrial, business, vocational, technical, home economics, music, and adult education courses.*

The essence of this regulation is that in federally assisted schools, all programs, including physical education, must be offered to males and females without regard to the gender of the students.

This legislation carried with it the mandate that all affected schools be in compliance with its provisions by July 21, 1978. A degree of controversy surrounded the implementation of Title IX, and several sets of guidelines were published by the Department of Health, Education, and Welfare in order to expedite the compliance process.

---

*Secs. 901, 902, Education Amendments of 1972, 86 Stat. 373, 374; 20 U.S.C., 1681, 1682.

The primary intent of Title IX, however, requires no legal interpretation. The law clearly states that all school programs must be coeducational. How has this requirement affected physical education programs? How has it affected other programs offered by secondary schools? Since physical educators do not operate in a vacuum and must be involved with the whole student in the total school setting, it is appropriate to consider Title IX and coeducational physical education with reference to facets of education that are common to all areas of the curriculum.

Boys and girls learning together.

Curricular revision

The impact of coeducation on the curricula of secondary schools is of great interest to physical educators. Although coeducational programs have existed for several years, curricular revision has developed slowly and has not demonstrated an easily identifiable pattern. Theoretically, there are several possible directions for secondary school physical education programs to take as the result of Title IX implementation.

One option is that physical education programs remain static, and educators make no curricular revisions for the accommodation of coeducational classes. If this approach is chosen, courses will be offered and conducted as usual, with the exception that males and females will participate in them together. Is this option realistic? Will this approach produce the desired results of coeducation? What are the advantages and disadvantages of maintaining the status quo?

Another approach that might be taken is to offer classes at various skill levels within the physical education curriculum. In this arrangement, students could

Coeducational cross-country skiing.

enroll in beginning, intermediate, or advanced sections of specific activities and participate with classmates of similar abilities. A variation of this approach would be to group the students according to their respective skill levels within given sections. In this situation, subgroups of beginning, intermediate, and advanced students would be identified within the context of the larger group. Does this approach offer any advantages to students? Are there administrative problems to consider? How could such a program be implemented?

Currently, individual and dual activities, recreative activities, and leisure-time pursuits are enjoying increased popularity. This emphasis on activities such as tennis, racketball, jogging, and dance has been accompanied by a decline of interest in traditional activities such as football, basketball, and other team sports. Secondary school physical education curricula might be revised to include these nontraditional activities. Would this approach to curricular revision enhance the physical education experiences of secondary school students? Could males and females participate side by side with positive results? Would students react favorably to this departure from tradition, or would they be resistant to such change? How might physical educators feel about altering the traditional curriculum? Would these new offerings fulfill the objectives of physical education?

As a physical educator, you may select one of the approaches presented, or you may develop additional options. In any case, the physical education programs in which you will teach probably will be coeducational. An understanding of the purposes of physical education and of the nature of the adolescent learner will be essential to the development of the most beneficial curricula.

Discipline

Discipline problems in secondary schools receive widespread publicity and attention. The introduction of mind-altering drugs into the lives of young people and the interpretation of personal freedom as it applies to school-aged youth have compounded these problems during recent years. Individuals considering teaching at the secondary school level should possess a realistic attitude toward the existence of discipline problems and be prepared to cope with them in positive ways.

Since coeducational physical education involves unique relationships between the sexes, it presents new considerations relative to discipline. Physical educators are concerned with two types of relationships that traditionally have not existed in the gymnasium—relationships between male and female students and relationships between teachers and students of the opposite sex.

Male and female adolescents may respond to coeducational physical education in various ways. They may adjust to the situation easily and proceed with their learning experiences in an orderly fashion. There is a possibility, however, that coeducation in the gymnasium will elicit some types of responses and behaviors that are not evident in classrooms traditionally shared by both sexes. Initial unfamiliarity with coeducational physical education may result in behavior requiring disciplinary action. What types of behavior might cause disruption of the daily routine? Might students taunt each other verbally? Could situations arise in which uneasiness with the opposite sex results in overt acts of physical abuse? Teenagers may be very sensitive to the concept of acquiring physical skills in the presence of the opposite sex, and they might react to their feelings of inadequacy with a degree of hostility and suspicion. What might physical educators do to encourage healthy relationships between the students and, thus, divert many discipline problems before they arise?

The reactions of students to physical educators of the opposite sex may also be varied. They may consider physical education teachers in much the same light as math or English teachers and be unconcerned about whether they are male or female. In this situation, discipline problems resulting from coeducation will be kept to a minimum. Some students, however, may resent physical educators of the opposite sex. They may be disdainful of their presence in what traditionally has been a single-sex setting. What types of discipline problems might be created by this attitude? What unique problems might arise when physical educators attempt to subdue students of the opposite sex?

To the majority of students, coeducational physical education will represent an opportunity for enrichment rather than an arena for the demonstration of sexual superiority. Others, usually those suffering from feelings of inferiority or insecurity, may view these experiences as threats to their self-concepts. It is essential that teachers of adolescents anticipate and understand the reactions of the students and deal with them accordingly. In most situations, knowledgeable, firm physical educators can create an atmosphere of mutual respect and trust that precludes an excess of displays of undesirable behavior.

Professional cooperation

Until the advent of Title IX, most secondary school physical education programs were segregated according to the gender of the students and teachers. With this arrangement, male and female physical educators frequently discharged their professional duties somewhat independently, with minimal interaction and coordination. Coeducation, however, has created a situation in which physical educators may combine their energies and talents and work together in mutual endeavors.

The necessity for cooperation between male and female physical educators has produced diverse results. In some circumstances, the transition has been beneficial to both the programs and the students and teachers involved. In other cases, however, programs have suffered while physical educators attempted to resolve personal and professional problems caused by this alteration of customary practice. The effects of coeducation on professional relationships among physical educators in secondary schools depend on each teacher's reaction to it. Professional, mature teachers who have the welfare of the students in mind should have little or no problem with coeducational physical education. Those teachers who have become accustomed to a traditional course of action and have no desire to either alter their teaching styles or share their time or facilities, however, may find the transition a harrowing experience.

How will you react to working with a physical educator of the opposite sex? Will you resent your counterpart or will you welcome the opportunity to work together? Do you possess predetermined notions about the professional competence of physical educators of the opposite sex, or are you receptive to the contributions of all educators?

As a prospective physical educator, you may wish to evaluate your feelings toward students and teachers of the opposite sex because ingrained attitudes, both positive and negative, tend to carry over into the classroom. If these attitudes are undesirable, they could serve to negate one of the primary potential benefits of coeducation—the development of sincere respect and appreciation of each sex for the other. Coeducation represents a refreshing opportunity for physical educators to cooperate both in principle and in practice and to work together toward the accomplishment of common goals.

Physical educators work as a team.

Humanism in the gymnasium

It may be safely assumed that most teachers consider themselves to be kind, compassionate human beings. In most instances, teachers attempt to maintain humanistic attitudes toward students even when faced with the tremendous social and professional stresses that occur during the course of a normal school day. Could coeducational physical education compound the pressures felt by physical educators? Might the presence of males and females in the same activity setting produce social and psychological problems that did not exist in single-sex classes? If so, what are these problems, and what might physical educators do to turn potential liabilities into assets?

A primary area of concern is the reaction of students to the physical prowess of the opposite sex. How might a highly skilled male react to being in a physical education class with a less-skilled female? And how might unskilled females feel about learning a physical skill in the same class as males? Might a highly skilled female feel self-conscious if she can perform at a higher level of skill than males? Will she continue to develop her abilities, or will she attempt to retard her progress because she does not wish to embarrass less-skilled males? Could the ego of the unskilled male suffer when some females evidence advanced levels of skill?

Answers to these questions will depend on the backgrounds and attitudes of individual students, and sensitive physical educators will be alert to the varying responses. As time passes, males and females will become more accustomed to participating together in the physical education setting. Until this occurs, however, and until traditional societal influences have been eradicated, psychological problems raised by coeducational physical education will continue to be among the primary considerations of secondary school physical educators.

A nontraditional physical education experience.

Another area of concern for the secondary school physical educator is the nature of the clothing required for many activities. In most circumstances, physical education attire is somewhat scanty in comparison with the clothing students wear to other classes, and that might pose problems for physical educators and students. How do students feel about wearing the brief attire necessary for many activities? Are their attitudes toward clothes worn for physical education classes different from their attitudes toward their usual clothing?

Adolescents are experiencing a growing awareness of their bodies. Since they are developing at varying rates of progress, they are acutely aware of their physical assets and liabilities. Physical development is very important to teenagers and frequently is the source of embarrassment and frustration. They are constantly comparing their levels of development, and physical education clothing lends itself to a closer inspection of the differences existing among students. How do students react to these circumstances? Are they indifferent, embarrassed, self-conscious, or proud with respect to their physical attributes? Does coeducational physical education have an effect on their body images and, hence, on their self-concepts? In what ways might physical educators begin to resolve some of the problems created by the nature of the clothing required for activity?

Coeducational physical education may present additional psychological problems for students and teachers. Adolescents are complex individuals whose reactions cannot always be predicted. Positive solutions to these problems will depend, to a great extent, on the attitudes of physical educators toward coeducational classes. If teachers view coeducation as an opportunity for males and females to interact in situations reflective of life, physical education can represent a rewarding experience for the students. If teachers stress socialization and the development of mutual respect between the sexes, coeducational physical educa-

Dance—a natural coeducational activity.

tion may serve to reinforce students' self-confidence and to strengthen their interpersonal relationships. Skilled, concerned physical educators are essential if coeducation is to achieve the desired goal of life enrichment for all students.

SUMMARY

Title IX of the Education Amendments Act of 1972 mandated that all federally assisted schools must have coeducational physical education programs by July 21, 1978. This departure from tradition has created a degree of controversy and discussion within the profession. Although many physical educators have welcomed coeducation and have hailed it as an opportunity for enrichment, others have considered it an intrusion on long-established practice and have resisted its implementation.

Coeducation affects secondary school physical education programs in several ways. The most visible aspects of the influence of Title IX on physical education programs are in the areas of curricular revision, discipline, professional cooperation, and humanism in the gymnasium.

As you investigate the literature, you will discover that an interest in coeducational physical education is not a new phenomenon. You will read articles written as long ago as 1935 advocating this approach to secondary school physical education. Why has it taken so long for coeducational physical education to be accepted? Why was legislation required for it to become a reality? Perhaps through your reading, you will discover answers to many of the questions about coeducational physical education and begin to develop insight concerning this concept's impact on students, teachers, and programs.

1   COEDUCATION—KEY TO GOOD LIFE ADJUSTMENT*

By John McIntyre

The opening of a new high school is an opportune time for its physical educators to appraise their program in terms of student needs, both present and future. The increasing complexity of our society necessitates a program planned to provide physical education in its complete sense. Attention must be given to the social and emotional needs as well as the physical needs of our secondary school students.

COEDUCATION IMPORTANT

A well-adjusted individual does not limit his activities to those with his own sex. Boys and girls work together in other phases of their high school life. Shouldn't they play together for their present good and future happiness? Yes, coeducational activities are needed for a well-balanced phys-

*From Journal of Health, Physical Education, and Recreation **28**:31, December 1957.

ical education program, one which promotes good life adjustment.

A school opening is a good time to introduce coeducational activities. Approval, support, and cooperation can be gained from administrators, staff, students, and parents, if the life adjustment values are stressed. When members of both boys and girls departments work together with enthusiasm, a successful program can be assured. Folk, square, and social dancing, with instruction by both a man and a woman instructor, volleyball, softball, archery, golf, and badminton have proved to be appropriate coeducational activities. They may be offered once a week or on a daily basis for a block of several weeks. Instruction can be given when needed, but recreational activity should be foremost. After-school corecreational classes are also popular when sponsored by GAA or the Block Society.

DESIRABLE OUTCOMES

Desirable outcomes in life adjustment are many for both the present and the future. Opportunities for the students to become well-acquainted with both girls and boys in a play situation increase their feeling of "belonging," even in a large new school. This results in greater participation in the extracurricular activities from which comes much valuable experience. Real learning in the classroom is also increased, for students feel more comfortable in each other's presence and enter into discussion and learn through good group dynamics and committee work.

School dances are immediately a great success, for the students know how to dance, know each other, and have been taught the social courtesies. The skills which the students develop, particularly in social dancing, give them self-confidence and status in the peer groups, so important to security, happiness, and good adjustment in the adolescent years.

Information can be given to boys and girls on football and basketball from a spectator's point of view. Many students then come to school games and school spirit is furthered. This also brings about increased enjoyment of future leisure time.

Opportunities to have many regular associations with the opposite sex in play situations make for healthy boy-girl relationships and eliminate need for objectionable attention-getting behavior. Seeing each other in more situations promotes greater tolerance for all types of personalities with realization of varying abilities and limitations. All this gives a good basis for choosing a mate.

BETTER DEVELOPMENT

This program proves to be a real stimulus to greater physical achievement in the total physical education program. Both boys and girls show more desire to perfect their skills. They demonstrate more self-control, appropriate manners, and good sportsmanship. They are more careful of their appearance and speech. They learn and make use of the social graces. These outcomes are likely to carry-over to sound leisure-time activities.

The life adjustment program in physical education contributes in many ways to the general and specific objectives of physical education, and thus to the better development of the whole student. The total educational program of a high school is improved when coeducational physical education is a well-functioning part.

2 COMPLIANCE WITH TITLE IX IN SECONDARY SCHOOL PHYSICAL EDUCATION*

By Don E. Arnold
Assistant Professor of Physical Education, University of Illinois at Urbana-Champaign, Urbana, Illinois

Secondary schools must bring their physical education and athletics programs into compliance with Title IX as soon as possible, but no later than July 21, 1978. It is emphasized that schools may only take advantage of the adjustment period where they can show real barriers to immediate compliance. This article identifies facets of the task of achieving compliance in physical education and athletics in secondary schools as an aid to schools now involved in this process.

The first step toward compliance was the self-evaluation of physical education policies and practices, which should have been completed by July 21, 1976. The results of the self-evaluation should be used by the school in taking remedial steps to eliminate the effects of discrimination. The evaluation document must be made available to students, parents, and others for at least three years. The compliance agency, OCR, will review the reports, but it will probably be several years before each report is read. Pressure to make changes in policies and practices needed to be in compliance will, no doubt, come from parents or others within the school district before it comes from OCR. And because boys and girls physical education and athletics programs have traditionally been separate, school districts may find that more adjustments are necessary in these programs than in other areas of the curriculum.

This discussion is intended to provide assistance to schools as they move toward compliance. Official interpretations covering Title IX of the Education Amendments of 1972 come from the regional centers of the Office of Civil Rights (Department of Health, Education and Welfare), which was given responsibility both for drafting regulations to interpret the legislation and for providing direction to schools as they endeavor to be in compliance. State departments of education are also among the sources of information on compliance. Helpful publications, prepared by the Resource Center on Sex Roles in Education (1201 16th St., N.W., Washington, D.C. 20009), include the following: *Complying with Title IX: Implementing Institutional Self-evaluation* and *Complying with Title IX: The First Twelve Months*. AAHPER has published a special manual for the profession entitled *Complying with Title IX of the Education Amendments of 1972 in Physical Education and High School Sports Programs*.

The lingering ignorance regarding Title IX, the plethora of misinformation surrounding it, and the adamant resistance to change within some schools is cause for apprehension that the potential positive contribution of Title IX to physical education and athletic programs will not be realized. When the potentially positive effects of all of the possible, if not the probable, facets of implementation are considered, it is as easy to become optimistic as to be pessimistic.

GENERAL PROHIBITIONS

Except as noted in the following discussion, sex designations are to be removed from class schedules, activity areas, and budgets. Institutions must provide for the use of all facilities and equipment on a nondiscriminatory basis. Schools may continue to use the term "girls' gym" for purposes of identification, but the use of a gymnasium, pool, gymnastics area, etc. exclusively by one sex would be unacceptable. The facilities contained in separate locker and shower rooms and the services provided therein must be equal. Among the factors to take into consideration in determining whether facilities are equal would be

*From The Journal of Physical Education and Recreation **48**:19-22, January 1977.

the relative numbers of shower heads, toilets, hair dryers, and size of lockers.

Regulations mandate that policies and rules regarding such matters as attendance, dress, uniforms, showering, dressing time, etc. shall apply equally to both sexes. Any rules denoting standards of conduct and appearance, and disciplinary action which might result from violating them, must be the same for each sex. Criteria established for all awards must be the same for girls and boys. The quality and quantity of the awards and the method of presentation must also be comparable.

Staffing will reflect affirmative action programs containing validated predetermined standards for employment selection. Advertising vacancies for male or female physical education teachers could only be justified in limited circumstances; an announcement for a male or female might be acceptable if it included among the responsibilities, locker room supervision and the coaching of a contact sport. Scheduling classes and the distribution of extracurricular assignments must be done on a nondiscriminatory basis.

Title IX does not require that sex-segregated administrative units must be merged, although this is certainly the trend. Before combining units, institutions must develop affirmative action programs demonstrating how a merger can be effected in a nondiscriminatory manner. Forming sex integrated offices within newly combined units is recommended to speed actual integration of previously separate units. Segregated offices for male and female staff could be justified, particularly where toilet or shower facilities are attached, but there can be no discrimination in the size of the office and provision of supplies and equipment.

TITLE IX STIPULATIONS APPLICABLE TO INSTRUCTIONAL PHASE

Physical education classes must be sex integrated. Many colleges and universities instituted coeducational physical education basic instruction classes several years ago and were pleased to find them very attractive to students.

Sex integrated classes will increase the range of physical size and ability of students. This fact will be most critical in those attendance centers where classes already contain two or more age groups, i.e., sophomores and seniors. Scheduling boys and girls in the same classes should make it possible to reduce the number of classes containing two or more age levels. Increasing the range of students' sizes and abilities has impli-

cations for physical educators as they group students for instruction and competition, choose instructional strategies, select activities, supervise, and evaluate student performance.

Whenever one sex predominates in a particular class, the school district should be prepared to explain the sex ratio of the class. Scheduling practices, overt exclusion (unless the activity being taught is a contact sport), and coercive student counseling are unacceptable explanations for having a predominance of one sex in a class. Designating certain sections of a multi-section course for single sex instruction would also be unacceptable. If interest in a particular activity is not shared equally by both sexes or if the activity is a contact sport, classes composed primarily of members of one sex are not in contravention of Title IX. Some schools may wish to take precautions such as not listing the name of the instructor with a particular class to avoid the charge of having influenced students in the selection of classes at registration.

Students may be grouped by ability where skills are assessed by objective standards of individual performance which are developed and applied without regard to sex. Students may also be segregated on the basis of sex for participation in contact sports, but only within the same area. Six sports are currently classified as contact sports—boxing, wrestling, ice hockey, football, basketball, and rugby, plus "other sports which involve bodily activity as its purpose or major activity." To get an additional sport designated as a contact sport, a written description of the sport indicating the extent to which its purpose or major activity involves bodily contact must be sent to the regional OCR. The decision will be made by the Washington headquarters. Title IX permits, but does not require, separation of the sexes for participation in contact sports. It requires sex integrated instruction in contact sports and then permits separation of the sexes for competition.

It is not necessary that instructors use a complicated or sophisticated means of grouping students for instruction or competition even in noncontact activities where possibilities of collision are present. A common sense standard is usually adequate. For example, having a 110-pound girl compete with a 210-pound boy *or* girl in activities where collision is possible is neither educationally sound nor likely to be judicially permissible. Classifications could be based upon one or more valid determinants of performance, such as height and strength.

The responsibility of school districts in most states is to provide a physical education program for all students including those unable to participate in the regular activity program. In view of Title IX a school district may wish to establish a policy of requiring a physician's certificate indicating the appropriate physical education experience whenever any apparent physical or mental condition, including pregnancy, raises some question as to the student's fitness for physical education.

Title IX will influence the selection of activities. The regulations preclude requiring members of one sex to take a specific activity (or any course for that matter) without requiring the opposite sex to also take the activity. If, for example, girls must take "slimnastics," then boys must also take that activity. If instruction in an activity is desirable, the requirement could be revised and instead of requiring a specific course, students could be allowed to select from a group of courses listed under headings such as fitness activities or combatives.

Selection of activities must reflect consideration for the needs and interests of boys and girls. It must be recognized that there is a large number of games and sports and dances from which to choose and no one activity is essential to the achievement of the objectives of physical education. Most activities currently utilized in the separate programs are suitable for coed participation, although utilization of certain of the activities will require careful grouping and perhaps some rule modification. Intramural programs, particularly at the college level, have been the proving grounds for innovative forms of dual and team coed competition. Tennis, volleyball, and other sports, including some classified as contact sports, are among those activities which have been used quite successfully. Rule modification need not be offensive to either sex. For example, asking boys to bat left-handed would not please either sex. However, a "no-slide" rule would decrease the chances of a collision and hence make play safer without offending either sex.

Because sex integrated classes generally contain a wider range of abilities and sizes, there is a greater risk of injury in those activities where there is the possibility of collision. Injury prevention must be a major concern as Title IX is implemented. Classes having a greater risk of injury must be more closely supervised. This does not necessarily mean more supervisors; it could mean a more structured class. It means strict enforcement of the rules by officials. Admittedly, some of the solutions to the problem of supervision that will be used during the transition period will prove unsatisfactory and temporary. However, a good faith effort will either produce a solution or provide justification for whatever temporary practice is being followed.

The responsibility for supervision includes the locker room; however, this supervision could be among the responsibilities of teacher aides, paraprofessionals, or teachers from other departments. Locker rooms may need to be added to the schedule drawn up to provide supervision in the wash rooms, halls, lunch room, etc.

There is ample precedent without our profession for instructors and coaches of one sex successfully supervising, teaching, and coaching teams composed of members of the opposite sex. Physical educators have also successfully met the challenge of supervising individualized programs and some of these were coed. The continuance of such programs shows that the profession has developed supervisory techniques adequate for new situations in the past and is expected to be able to do so again.

It is anticipated that many schools, particularly those with larger staffs, will form instructional teams consisting of at least one member of each sex to teach their sex integrated classes. Choosing this alternative enables schools to realize the benefits of team teaching, simplifies scheduling, and allows for adequate supervision.

Individualizing instruction is an effective way of accommodating the wide range of abilities which may be expected when classes become coed. Coupling this approach with team teaching and individualized evaluation largely eliminates obstacles to being in compliance in the instructional phase.

Schools which choose, or are forced, to assign only one teacher to its sex integrated classes can still be in compliance. This is true even though formal or structured teaching methods are utilized. The instructor of such classes, and there will be many, has to be particularly careful in selecting activities and in grouping, supervising, and evaluating students.

Schools with small staffs can meet compliance standards even though they cannot or do not choose to form instructional teams. These schools could perhaps best utilize the competencies of individual staff members and most effectively accommodate the needs and interests of students by making shorter term teaching assignments. The male and female teachers could exchange or rotate class schedules and preparation times so that their expertise is available to students scheduled each class period.

It is understandable that compliance conversation among physical educators frequently focuses upon evaluating students. Marking has always been a challenge and Title IX has, in the eyes of many physical educators, made the challenge more formidable. Marks should reflect progress toward course objectives and may be based upon achievement, i.e., present status; growth, i.e., change or gain; or a combination of both.

Since the Title IX regulations require that objective standards of individual performance be developed and applied without regard to sex, Title IX supports the position that marks should reflect the progress students have made in relation to their own abilities. Where marks are based on growth, the objective standard of skill performance may be the student's previous performance. Comparing a student's performance to a single norm is permissible only where its application does not adversely affect members of one sex. If a standard is used and its application to girls is unfair because boys are generally taller and stronger, separate standards for girls must be used. Most, if not all of the most frequently used fitness, motor ability, and skill tests are sex based. Their norms could be used to aid teachers in gauging individual growth.

It is probably that Title IX will also influence the method used to report pupil progress. Title IX encourages individual grading and it is hoped that more schools will adopt the method of preparing written statements, diagnostic and prescriptive in nature, which reflect progress toward course objectives. However, the regulations place increased emphasis on subjective evaluation. More physical educators may decide that they are left with insufficient objective data with which to discriminate between an "A" and a "B" without spending an unreasonable amount of time in class as well as outside on evaluation. As a result, more schools may utilize a two-symbol system.

TITLE IX STIPULATIONS APPLICABLE TO INTRAMURALS AND ATHLETICS

Clearly, Title IX legislation will have a profound impression upon athletic programs at all levels. The regulations and comments preceding them reflect OCR's position that athletics are an integral part of the educational program and, as such, are fully subject to Title IX regulations even when athletic programs do not receive federal funds directly.

Title IX requires that each sex shall have equal opportunity to participate in intramurals and interscholastic programs. Exactly what constitutes equal opportunity is not defined in the regulations. Among those factors to be considered in making such a determination are the following: whether the selection of sports and levels of competition effectively accommodate the interests and abilities of members of both sexes, provision of equipment and supplies, scheduling of games and practice and competitive facilities, publicity, and insurance coverage available to athletes.

The regulations do not require equal expenditures for each team or equal aggregate expenditures, although this information might well be one of several pieces of data studied to determine whether equal access to inter-scholastic and intramural opportunities is being provided.

Schools may offer separate teams in the contact sports and in those sports where selection is based upon competitive skill. Schools are required to offer separate teams only when sponsorship of primarily girls and boys teams is the only way to effectively accommodate the interests and abilities of both sexes. If a school sponsors separate teams, selection must be based on competitive skill. Members of one sex may be allowed to try out for the team sponsored for members of the opposite sex.[1] This interpretation rejects the separate but equal position. The separate but equal concept has been declared unacceptable by the courts in other areas of the educational program, but there was widespread support for the applicability of this concept to interscholastic programs.

Neither sex has the right to participate on a contact sport team sponsored for members of the opposite sex, even though it is the only school team in that sport. If there are enough members

---

[1]The wording in the manual developed by HEW for use in regional offices, on this point, is: "A recipient may operate unitary teams (i.e., teams composed of members of both sexes) for which selection is based upon competitive skill only if, in doing so, the interests and abilities of members of both sexes are effectively accommodated. In other words, where a school decides that anyone, regardless of sex, may try out for a team, and there is substantial interest on the part of females in that sport, but very few members of that sex have skill sufficient to be selected, the sponsorship of the unitary team would not be sufficient to meet the interests and abilities of both sexes."

of the excluded sex who want to compete and if there have been fewer opportunities for that sex to participate in interscholastic athletics, the school is obligated to sponsor a team for the excluded sex. Schools could permit coed competition in contact sports if they chose to do so.

If a school sponsors a team in a noncontact sport for members of one sex and does not sponsor a team in that sport for members of the other sex, members of the excluded sex must be allowed to try out for that team if over-all athletic opportunities for members of the excluded sex have previously been limited. The mere fact that a school sponsors only a girls or boys team does not give members of the opposite sex the privilege of trying out. The cross-over privilege would exist only where the opportunities for participation in interscholastic competition have been limited for the excluded sex.

A school may sponsor a single team open to members of both sexes where selection is based on competitive skill; however, the single team must effectively accommodate the interests and abilities of members of both sexes. A school which sponsors a team in any contact or noncontact sport and allows both sexes to try out, is still in contravention of Title IX if there is substantial interest among females but very few females have sufficient skills to be selected. This situation would indicate that separate teams are needed.

If a school sponsors one team in a sport open to both sexes, the coach has the responsibility of using objective criteria to select who competes. Utilization of a performance-based criterion would seem to be a logical choice. In individual sports such as golf, cross-country, and singles play in tennis, the winners in intra-squad competition would represent the school in interscholastic contests. Of course, the coach's task of selecting players in team sports such as volleyball and softball is more difficult. However, the coach who engages in a good faith effort to select team members on the basis of ability will undoubtedly be faced with fewer charges of discrimination. If a coach's judgment is questioned, he/she may find it confirmed by squad members or by whatever means of selection is suggested by those who made the challenge.

When determining whether or not individuals may cross-over or whether a school is obligated to sponsor separate teams, it is previous rather than present athletic opportunities which should receive the most attention. Present opportunities are supposed to be equal; at least they must be equal by the end of the adjustment periods. A comparison of athletic opportunities must be based on total programs rather than competitive outlets in a specific sport.

In most instances, cross-over privileges will be extended to girls only, since previous opportunities for girls to participate in interscholastic competition have been more limited than those afforded boys. Authority for the preference shown to girls is found in the definition of affirmative action contained in the regulations. Obviously, there is a fine line between acceptable affirmative action and unacceptable reverse discrimination. OCR has not yet provided any guidelines for distinguishing between the two nor does it specify how long schools are to engage in affirmative action programs.

The regulations imply that teams composed primarily or exclusively of one sex may not be denied the services of an athletic trainer of the opposite sex.

Where a school sponsors separate teams in a sport, the length of seasons and number of contests must be comparable. Schools may offer the same sport at different times of the year for boys and girls, and contests may be played on different days and times during the season. However, opportunities to compete before an audience should be comparable.

Schools may not pay coaches of one sex less than that paid to coaches of the opposite sex for equal work on jobs the performance of which requires equal skill, effort and responsibility and which are performed under similar working conditions (pressure). Among other factors to consider in setting defensible compensation for coaches of either sex are length of seasons, number of players, size of staff, and preseason and postseason responsibilities.

COST OF COMPLIANCE

The cost of compliance in physical education, intramurals, and athletics is a primary concern at all levels of education and it is difficult to even estimate the cost without first identifying the plan to achieve it. Each district is unique and must develop its own plan to achieve congruence with Title IX (a fact recognized in the regulations). Although costs will vary from school district to school district, some general observations can be made.

The fact that more and more school boards are finding it increasingly difficult to balance budgets lessens the possibility of schools solving compliance problems by adding staff, facilities, and equipment. It seems probable that some valid arguments for solutions of this nature exist. If schools were doing a reasonably good job of physically educating boys and girls prior to July 21, 1975, merely combining these programs should not significantly increase costs. Consequently, in most instances it would be difficult to justify additional expenditures for physical education even if monies were available.

The budgetary effect of adding or expanding a girls athletic program could range from not increasing the present athletic budget at all to doubling it. The cost of the total athletic program would not increase if the boys program were scaled down in direct proportion to the amounts of money needed to fund girls interscholastics and intramurals. Doubling the present budget would enable a school to initiate or expand a girls program to the level of the boys program, but few schools would have the money or facilities to offer such a program. There are probably few schools where the interests and abilities of the girls in intramurals and athletics would justify such a step at this time.

SUMMARY

Grouping students for instruction and competition, choosing instructional strategies, selecting activities, supervising, and evaluating student performance are recognized responsibilities of the physical educator. Teaching coed classes may require that the teacher meet these responsibilities somewhat differently. However, it is emphasized that these legal and moral responsibilities must still be met in a reasonably prudent manner. The standard against which the conduct of the defendant in negligence litigation will be measured is not likely to be less stringent because of the need to comply with Title IX.

Title IX will make a profound impression upon interscholastic athletic programs at all levels. It is emphasized that the legislation requires equal opportunity, not equal programs. Title IX stipulates that the obligation to sponsor separate teams and cross-over rights exists only in situations where previous opportunities to participate in interscholastic programs of the excluded sex have been more limited than those of the opposite sex.

Clearly, spending a disproportionate amount of the budget for the instructional phase of the physical education program on one sex or the other violates the regulations. Spending 80-90% of the athletic budget on the boys can no longer be justified on the basis of tradition. It might be justified where a girls program requiring only 10% of the total budget for athletics and intramurals effectively accommodated the needs and interests of the girls. This would be unusual even today, and it will probably grow more unlikely every year.

Physical education programs can make a considerable contribution to the continuation of the crucial socialization process initiated by the judiciary and by Congress. Instructional, intramural, and interscholastic programs have tremendous appeal for young people during their formative years. Consequently, these programs have good potential for stimulating the reexamination of the roles and statuses of males and females in contemporary society and for educating participants and followers in the wisdom and benefits of basic human equality. Physical educators and school administrators control the degree to which physical education and interscholastic athletics will contribute to this socialization process. The critical decisions regarding Title IX compliance should be made with this potential in mind.

SUPPLEMENTAL READINGS
1930-1939

3. Duggan, Anne Schley: Dance as a co-educational activity, The Journal of Health and Physical Education **10:**457-459, 488-489, October 1939.
4. Van Hagen, Winifred: What are the possibilities of coeducational physical education in secondary schools? The Journal of Health and Physical Education **6:**14-15, 56-57, September 1935.

1940-1949

5. Fait, Hollis F.: The case for corecreation, The Journal of the American Association for Health, Physical Education, and Recreation **20:**515, 555-557, October 1949.
6. Overton, Frank M., and Han, Clara Follick: Co-recreation at the university school, The Physical Educator **1:**69-71, December 1940.
7. Smith, Kenyon: Problems in developing and programming coeducational classes in junior high schools, The Physical Educator **1:**213-216, June 1941.

1950-1959

8. Overbey, William S.: Coeducational recreation in our schools, The Physical Educator **16:**10-11, March 1959.

1970-1979

9. Coulter, Bruce: Organizing a coeducational gymnastics course, The Journal of Physical Education and Recreation **49:**17-18, April 1978.
10. Elliott, Patricia A.: The beneficial outcomes of requiring coeducational programs, Journal of Health, Physical Education, and Recreation **43:**35-36, February 1972.
11. Johnson, Lee: Coed sports in high school, The Journal of Physical Education and Recreation **48:**23-25, January 1977.
12. Kelly, Barbara J.: Implementing Title IX, The Journal of Physical Education

and Recreation **48:**27-28, February 1977.
13. McGrath, Alice, and Tegner, Bruce: Coeducational self-defense, The Journal of Physical Education and Recreation **48:**28-29, January 1977.
14. Taylor, Bernie, and Mikols, Walter J.: Coed weight training, The Journal of Physical Education and Recreation **48:**22-23, June 1977.

ASSIGNMENTS
Individual activities

1. Select one article from each decade represented in the reading list and submit a paper comparing the various points of view toward coeducational physical education.
2. Select one article from each decade represented in the reading list and prepare a case for coeducational physical education in the secondary schools. Include problems that might be encountered and possible solutions to those problems.
3. Read article 2 and discuss its implications in class.
4. Invite a secondary school teacher to class to speak on coeducational physical education as it affects curricular revision, discipline, professional cooperation, and humanism in the gymnasium.

Group presentations

1. Drama
   a. TOPIC: *Benefits of coeducational physical education.*
   b. PARTICIPANTS: Physical educators representing various decades.
   c. FUNCTIONS: To enact a meeting in which the physical educators discuss the values of coeducational physical education at the secondary level, problems that might be encountered, and possible solutions to those problems.
   d. OBJECTIVES OF PRESENTATION: (1) To identify specific physical educators and time periods, (2) to identify desir-

able outcomes of coeducational physical education, (3) to identify problems and solutions, and (4) to illustrate similarities among opinions of earlier and contemporary physical educators.

e. ARTICLES: 1-14.

2. Panel discussion

a. TOPIC: *Coeducational physical education curriculum*.

b. PARTICIPANTS: Physical educators representing various decades; parents of secondary school students.

c. FUNCTIONS: To present a coeducational physical education curriculum at a meeting of a parents' and teachers' association; some of the parents are opposed to coeducational physical education.

d. OBJECTIVES OF PRESENTATION: (1) To identify specific physical educators and time periods, (2) to present the rationale supporting coeducational physical education, (3) to present some of the opposing arguments to such a program, (4) to present specific activities to be offered, and (5) to illustrate the consistency of opinion among earlier and contemporary physical educators.

e. ARTICLES: 1-14.

CHAPTER FOUR

Competitive athletics

"It is by no means, however, only the physical power that is fed and strengthened in these games."
Friedrich Fröbel, 1830

Controversies surrounding competitive athletics traditionally have generated much discussion and debate among physical educators. Although the profession of physical education encompasses many areas other than competitive sport and the goals and objectives of physical education extend far beyond the athletic arena, professional literature reveals that competitive athletics are a significant part of our heritage. The precise nature of the relationship between physical education and athletics has never been clearly established, but a relationship of some type does appear to exist. The vast number of articles about competitive athletics that have been published in physical education literature support the contention that physical educators have been, and continue to be, deeply involved with and interested in the world of athletic competition.

Numerous issues exist in the realm of competitive athletics. This chapter is limited to discussions of four issues with which a physical educator is likely to be involved: (1) the objectives of competitive athletics, (2) the administrative organization of school athletic programs as they relate to physical education programs, (3) controversies surrounding childhood competitive athletics, and (4) competitive athletic programs for females. Although it is not the function of this chapter to provide you with easily memorized answers to the questions posed here, it is hoped that the questions will serve the purposes of stimulating your intellect and whetting your appetite for discovering the facts through the literature.

OBJECTIVES OF COMPETITIVE ATHLETICS

Observations of human beings throughout the centuries reveal that we possess an inherently competitive nature. Our personal experiences serve to illustrate the

Determination.

fact that competition among human beings is natural and is to be expected. As children, did not all of us hold contests in which we attempted to determine who could run the fastest, climb the highest, spell the most words correctly, outstare the other, hold one's breath the longest, and emerge victorious in many other forms of competition? Most of us also relate to competition as adults. There are values in competition, objectives worthy of pursuit; but controversy revolves around the precise nature of these objectives, the degree of emphasis that each should receive, and the most advantageous routes toward their attainment.

What *are* the objectives of athletic competition—particularly, interscholastic and intercollegiate athletics? The responses to that question are as varied as the opinions and experiences to which each individual has been exposed. Although the issue has been debated throughout the years, no clear-cut consensus has developed. Physical educators are deeply involved in the frequently painful process of determining the true values of interscholastic and intercollegiate athletic competition. As a future physical educator, coach, administrator, or parent, how do you view the contributions of competitive athletics to the lives of young people? Do athletics build character, and if they do, is this character desirable or undesirable? Is winning an objective of competition? Is it the only valid objective?

Self-discipline is essential for success in athletics.

Are sportsmanship and a sense of fair play developed through participation in competitive athletics? Is this development guaranteed? What is the function of the coach in the quest for these objectives? Are the qualities of emotional control, cooperation, good attitudes, and pride in excellence encouraged through participation in competitive athletics? Are good health and physical fitness realistic outcomes of an athletic program? Must spectators be entertained, and to what degree should they affect the nature of athletic programs? To what extent should athletic programs serve as a portion of the public relations program for a school or university? Are there scientifically sound and realistically formulated principles on which we can base our convictions about the objectives of competitive athletics?

There are no universally accepted answers to these questions. It will be necessary for you to study the literature and arrive at your own conclusions, and you should be able to defend your position, regardless of what it may be. The day has come and gone when meaningless clichés about the values of athletic competition are sufficient to satisfy the public. In today's climate of accountability, students, parents, and taxpayers demand justification for the existence of interscholastic and intercollegiate athletic programs. They will look to physical educators and athletic program personnel to provide that justification.

As you read the literature, you might keep an open mind and remember that everyone has had somewhat different experiences in athletics. Opinions are closely tied with personal experience, but they should not be allowed to operate independently of rational thought and logic. Perhaps the messages of the scholars in this area will provide information and insight that will equip you to determine some of the values that can be claimed for interscholastic and intercollegiate athletics.

THE RELATIONSHIP BETWEEN ATHLETIC AND PHYSICAL EDUCATION PROGRAMS

The second controversy in competitive athletics involves the administrative organization of school athletic programs as they relate to physical education programs. Should athletic programs be included as a part of physical education programs, or should they be administered separately? Should physical education teachers also be coaches, or should the coaches be selected from among other teachers in the school? Are there similarities between the objectives of athletics and the objectives of physical education? Are athletics curricular or extracurricular? How will the answers to these questions affect the manner in which athletic programs are financed and administered?

The literature reveals various opinions about the relationship between athletic and physical education programs. When you accept your first teaching position, you probably will have little to say about the organization and administration of athletics and physical education; however, as you grow and mature professionally, you may be called on to provide knowledgeable leadership in this area. In

Not all of the action is on the field.

order for you to provide such leadership, you should be aware of the advantages and disadvantages of the various options available. Regardless of whether you are actively involved in athletics, it is essential to recognize the fact that as a physical educator, you will affect the athletic program and the athletic program will affect you. In most school situations, the physical education program and personnel are aligned with the athletic program in such a way that understanding and cooperation are vital to the effectiveness of both programs.

The reading that you will do in this area will introduce you to various methods of organization and administration of athletic programs and physical education programs. You will be afforded opportunities to supplement your present frame of reference with new ideas and to begin developing personal convictions about the relationship between athletic programs and physical education programs.

What's the verdict?

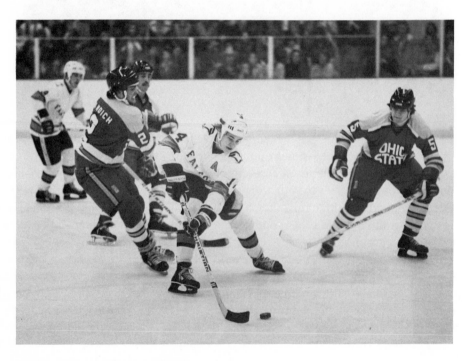

Interschool rivalry is frequently intense.

CHILDHOOD ATHLETICS

The third controversy in athletics concerns the age level at which organized competition should begin. As you probably know, opportunities for organized competition for young children are abundant. Is this a new phenomenon? You will find through your study that the issue of athletic competition for children of elementary school age—and younger—has been a vigorously debated topic for many years. The time will come, however, when you will no longer be able to view the controversy as a bystander. You will have sons, daughters, nieces, nephews, and students who may express a desire to participate in this competition. As a physical educator, you may be able to offer advice and furnish evidence supporting your position. You may be certain that you will be expected to have an opinion—an opinion based on facts.

What are the facts? Who knows whether Little League or other forms of organized childhood athletics are helpful or harmful, and on what criteria should such determinations be made? What are the objectives of organized competition for children, and why did highly organized programs develop? Would spontaneous neighborhood play produce equal joy and exhilaration for the child, and do all children have access to neighborhood play? How important are the physical, mental, and emotional levels of maturity of the children? How significant are the attitudes and ambitions of the parents of the participants? Who should provide the leadership for these programs? Should athletic programs for children be sponsored by the schools or by other agencies? What qualifications should the coaches be expected to possess?

Many questions surround organized competitive athletic programs for children, and they may seem to be overwhelming. It would be ideal to be able to furnish you with a list of answers but, as with many other areas, no concrete answers exist. In searching for answers through the literature, the most important consideration must be an objective appraisal of the facts in light of the welfare of the children involved.

ATHLETIC PROGRAMS FOR FEMALES

The fourth issue revealed in the literature is that of organized athletic competition for females. Opinions on this topic are diverse. Should women participate in full-blown, big-time athletic programs or in no competition at all? Should those professionals involved in physical education and athletics compromise by sponsoring intramurals and perhaps a few extramural or varsity events? Perhaps women should be content with *playdays,* events that were popular with our foremothers.

As you research the topic, you may want to consider the following questions: Why did athletic programs for males and athletic programs for females develop in such different ways? What are traditional societal attitudes toward females? Why are teams comprising males referred to as *men's teams* or *school* or *university*

Reaching for that extra effort.

teams while teams comprising females are referred to as *girls' teams* or, worse yet, are accorded the dubious honor of being known as the *Tigerettes, Lionettes,* or some similar indicator of diminutive stature? What is happening in women's athletics today—and why? What impact has Title IX had on competitive athletic programs for females? What impact has Title IX had on athletic programs for males? Are current developments wholesome or detrimental to the purposes of athletics? It may astonish you to discover that there was a time in our recent history when athletic programs for women were widespread and popular. What happened? Why did opinions and programs change, and why has the tide of opinion once again turned?

These questions represent only a few of the issues surrounding athletic programs for females. Additional considerations include: traditional concepts of femininity and masculinity, the needs and desires of female athletes, the physical and competitive potentials of females, and the budgetary effects of programs for females on the deeply entrenched programs for males.

The literature concerning athletic programs for females is fascinating and enlightening. Hopefully, you will enjoy learning of the history of athletic programs

Confrontation on the court.

for women, the strengths and weaknesses of females, female athletic potential, and the predicted future of competitive athletic programs for women.

SUMMARY

As you move into the professional realm, you may discover that you are discontent with certain qualities and characteristics of particular athletic programs or with the total concept of athletic programs as you find them administered in the schools. You may, on the other hand, find the situation compatible with your philosophy and principles. In either case, you will be in a position to affect the future of athletic programs and the benefits that the participants may derive from

Fitness and power at the net.

them. Your influence may be among the factors that chart the course of athletic programs for generations to come.

The four primary issues existing in competitive athletics are: (1) the objectives of competitive athletics, (2) the administrative organization of school athletic programs as they relate to school physical education programs, (3) controversies surrounding childhood competitive athletics, and (4) competitive athletic programs for females. The literature reveals diverse opinions relative to these issues, and a thorough investigation of the facts is essential for leading you to the establishment of personal and professional convictions. In the limited time available in a single course, it will not be possible for you to acquire all of the knowledge desirable in each area; however, through your reading, you may gain a sense of the issues and should develop a thirst for knowledge that will influence you to pursue these topics in depth.

1 AEL'S FABLES: PHILOSOPHICAL FANTASIES FOR PHYSICAL EDUCATION*

By Louis E. Alley
University of Iowa

Once upon a time there lived, deep in a primeval forest, a colony of spiders. Now these spiders were just the ordinary run of spiders. Probably a careful study and classification of them would have shown that by far the most of them were alike within the limits of their individual idiosyncrasies.

One thing they had in common, however, which was apparent to even the most casual observer. Those spiders were happy, as happy as spiders could be! They were happy because they kept themselves busy during their spare time spinning webs, webs of all sizes and patterns which hung from every branch and leaf.

HAPPY JUST SPINNING

Somehow the spinning of a web just made a spider happy. His spider heart would seem to sing in harmony with the forest about him as he spun his web in an intricate design which was all his own. He knew that his web would trap flies and other insects which would appease his pangs of hunger, but that wasn't what made him happy. It was just spinning the web that did it, somehow.

If he had been a modern, educated spider he might have attributed this glow of happiness and feeling of well-being, which attended the spinning of his web, to the satisfaction of an innate urge to create. He might have known, also, that the spinning brought about certain physiological changes in his body which stimulated the functioning of particular essential organs and glands and made him a healthier spider. But he didn't know all that. He just spun and was happy!

One fine, happy day one of the more intelligent spiders happened to notice that a particular web was just a little bit more attractive than all the other webs. The threads were just a little finer,

and the geometric pattern was just a bit more intricate. Not much, you understand, but just a little. Being an intelligent spider, he was curious, and asked the creator of the web to tell him his secret.

The spinner of the web was quite flattered and willingly demonstrated how he did it. In practically no time at all, the intelligent spider caught on and was spinning a web quite as good as the first, perhaps even a little better. Other spiders noticed the unusual webs and, hearing of the success of the intelligent spider, asked for instruction, demonstration and guidance, and many of them learned to spin the "new" web.

SPINNING BETTER WEBS

This startling development caused such a furor among the spider colony that the topic came up for discussion at the following meeting of the spider council. After much debate the council, which was composed of the older, wiser spiders, decided that a group of the better web-spinners should be employed for the specific purpose of teaching others how to spin more attractive webs.

In order that they might devote full time to their teaching, and to the study of the problem of improving web-spinning, each of them was to be paid the sum of ten flies and one mosquito per day—not a magnificent salary, to be sure, but adequate. Only the most skillful spinners of the colony were selected and appointed to the positions, with the exception of one spider who, though quite an ordinary spinner, happened to be a third cousin, by marriage, of the governor of the spider council.

The success of the program was a wonder to behold. By combining their talents and giving serious consideration to the problem, the teacher-spiders were able to discover many new and different ways of spinning webs—webs of such fragility and intricacy that they almost defied the imagination. Of course, only a few of the most gifted and more highly intelligent spiders could

*From The Journal of the American Association for Health, Physical Education, and Recreation **25:**6, 45, June 1954.

spin such webs. The vast majority of the spiders improved to some extent, but the work of only a few could be termed sensational.

True, the webs they spun were not any better for catching flies than any of the others. Neither did their creation change, or in any way improve the physiological effects of the web spinning upon the individual spider. The spiders were not any happier as a result of the improved web spinning; in fact, there was a tendency for each to be hypercritical of his own handiwork and of that of others. Critical examination was almost certain to uncover some tiny flaw, and its discovery would inevitably cause the spinner to be slightly dissatisfied with his creation. But, no doubt about it, some of those spiders could *really* spin a wicked web.

WEB-SPINNING CONTESTS

Now, the teacher-spiders became deeply engrossed in developing student-spiders who could spin outstanding webs. They organized annual colony-wide web-spinning contests in which all the better web-spinners from even the most remote areas of the colony came to spin. Their craftsmanship was evaluated in terms of uniqueness, intricacy, fragility, and general geometric harmony, and a grand champion spinner was determined.

Until the next year's contest was held, this champion was quite a colony figure, being banqueted upon the choice flies and mosquitoes of the forest. Small spiders admired, even worshiped, him and dreamed of the day when they, too, might be champion. Such was the clamor and hubbub over the annual champion webspinner that the spider-teachers grew to be constantly alert for young spiders who showed particular promise and, upon finding such spiders, would spend hours and hours in developing their talents.

A spider-teacher's ability to teach web spinning came to be judged in terms of the products turned out by his most apt pupil, and, it was rumored, some of the teachers who instructed the most successful spinners received as much as ten extra flies per month! It was further whispered in quiet tones that they, in turn, gave *some* of the ten flies to their prize pupils. (The amount the pupils received was never definitely established, but there was the rumor.)

A number of the old "mossback" spiders muttered in their spider-beards at the general state of affairs and made belittling comments concerning

the younger generation, but nobody paid any attention. After all, the web spun by the champion of each annual web-spinning contest was far superior to any web spun in the old days, as any fool could see.

SOMETHING WRONG

Well, you know, along about this time a sort of undefinable pall of something or other settled down on the entire colony of spiders. It was hard to put a finger on just what was the matter. *Something* was wrong, and all of the spiders *knew* something was wrong, but none of the spiders knew *what* was wrong. Perhaps it could be best described as a general state of uneasiness. That old feeling of happiness, of being in harmony with the whole forest, had somehow vanished. Things just weren't quite right anymore.

Now, if those spiders had been particularly alert and observing, they might have noticed that a vast majority of spiders weren't spinning webs any more. Oh, sure, they spun a little bit. They had to, in order to keep life and limb together. After all, they had to catch something to eat, so they spun just enough of a web to do just that and then withdrew into a "web-cave" which they spun in the center. There they spent their days, venturing out only to seize any hapless victims which became entangled in their webs and to drag them back into their caves.

One can halfway excuse the spiders for not noticing this because all of the very young spiders were out spinning furiously. However, a really close examination would have shown that as soon as a young spider realized that his web did not compare with those of the gifted spiders, and that it probably never would, he quit spinning for all but practical purposes, and withdrew into his web-cave to await his next meal. This realization probably first struck him when he noticed that the spider-teachers weren't spending much time with him, at least not as much as with a few spiders who spun webs which made him look extremely poor.

WHAT WAS WRONG

If those spiders had been educated spiders, versed in the knowledge of psychology, physiology, kinesiology, and all the rest of the "ologies," they would, undoubtedly, have known what was wrong. With only a few of the spiders spinning, and by far the greater number spending their days in their caves, it is easy for you and me to understand what caused the uneasiness which covered the colony like a cloud of misery. It could have easily been explained in terms of the physiology of web-spinning, or even in terms of the regenerating effects of creating, or recreation, but the spiders didn't know all that so the gloom settled deeper and deeper.

You don't believe me? Well, you just watch spiders, even today. When you see one, he will be doing one of two things. He'll either be way back in his web-cave, in the center of his web, just sitting and waiting, or he will be out spinning feverishly, almost madly. When you see one out spinning, take a good look at that nervous, quick-acting gentleman. For all you know, he may be the future champion web-spinner in the coming annual web-spinning contest!

MORAL: *Isn't it fortunate that people have more sense than spiders!*

---

2 STATUS OF SPORTS IN CONTEMPORARY AMERICAN SOCIETY*

By Robert Singer**

The status of sports and athletics has been subject to much debate ever since the early and late Athenian periods (776-355 B.C.), and possibly even before then. The Olympic games, begun in 776 B.C., and supposedly representative of the highest in ideals and athletics, had to be finally dissolved in 394 A.D. because the Games were no longer games. Athletics of the period, once the symbol of the highest achievement, had been degraded, misused, and made worthless with the decadence of the great Greek civilization.

Many years passed before sports and athletics were again to come to the attention of people. Interest grew slowly in the nineteenth century. The first intercollegiate competition (rowing) occurred in America in 1852. This was followed by baseball (1857), football in the 1860's, and others soon after. The Olympics were renewed in 1896 in Athens, and the United States was represented at this event.

At the turn of the century intercollegiate football became so unmanageable that the Intercollegiate Athletic Association (I.A.A.) was formed in 1905. Five years later, the name of the Association was changed to the National Collegiate Athletic Association (N.C.A.A.), and this Association still exists, exerting powerful control over intercollegiate competition in practically all sports.

It is interesting that the Greeks, as well as contemporary civilizations, have found sports productive of evil as well as good, pleasure and dissatisfaction. In general, it has been and is a source of controversy. Whereas the Olympics had to be dissolved in the olden days, and athletics practically forbidden throughout the Dark and Middle Ages, modern sports, under the guidance and with the assistance of many controlling bodies, notably the N.C.A.A., A.A.U., N.A.I.A., and the N.F.S.H.S.A.A., have won a new height of acclaim and attention at the present time. Because of the publicity, emphasis, and control of sport, the situation has become as distasteful to some people as it is popular with others.

The limitations and assets of sport should be realized by coaches, players, spectators, educators, family, and the public in general. Weaknesses must be overcome and controversial areas ironed out. Many people are not aware of the contributions of sport to the total development of the participants. These, too, must be acknowledged and used for effective promotion of a program of athletics.

Let us look at some of the assets of sport and the contribution it makes to the quality of American living. Since sport is subject to criticism some of these objections will be presented as well.

*From The Physical Educator **23:**147-149, December 1966.
**Dr. Singer, an assistant professor at Illinois State University, Normal, gives us a bird's eye view of some problems in sports.

ASSETS OF SPORTS

1. *Sports provide the more athletically gifted people with a means of developing their skills even further.* The educational system of our country is supposed to offer a program which encompasses the needs and interests of all the students. There are programs for physically handicapped youngsters, and those individuals low in physical fitness and/or motor ability are provided with additional assistance. The need for sports as an outlet for the gifted cannot be denied.

2. *Nowhere in education can a student's values be more directly influenced than in the keen competition of sport.* One of the primary roles of education is to inculcate values and morals in students so that they will lead more useful lives. A coach who maintains a high sense of values can exert a beneficial influence on his team members. Daily practice sessions and actual contests produce close contact between coach and players and create situations with rich educational implications. Honesty, the ability to win and lose graciously, fair play, ethics, leadership, spirit, etc.—these are a few of the many character traits which can and should be developed in each player under the guidance of the coach.

3. *Personal relationship was one of the four objectives of education set down by the Educational Policies Commission in 1938. Sports,* with special reference to team sports, *have a major role to contribute to this goal.* Boys (or girls) have to play together, to be together, think together—they have to be an organized unit if the team is to function best. Transfer from the sport's situation may possibly carry over to many transactions in life.

4. *An athletic event which represents a particular school will tend to create spirit in that school.* Call it a spirit of nationalism, if you will. The contest not only involves and arouses the students of the schools or colleges involved, but also residents of the town, city, and even state. People take pride in their team. The team is a sort of "common ground" for many persons of all ages with diversified interests and vocations. The athletic contest brings out the feelings of people: their spirit, enthusiasm, and pride.

5. *Finally, sports will better develop the physical fitness of the participants.* A strong body, functioning maximally along with an active and stimulated mind, is the ideal condition for which most of us strive. Through conditioning practices, athletes have the opportunity to develop themselves beyond a mediocre state.

LIABILITIES OF SPORTS

1. *The present role of athletics* in our society has resulted in an overemphasis on recruiting of athletes in many colleges and universities throughout the land. In many cases, academic standards are lowered for their benefit and illegal monetary rewards are given to these prodigies. The situation reached such a bleak point in the collegiate ranks in 1948, that the N.C.A.A. was impelled to enforce the "Sanity Code." Although it was not officially in effect long, due to loud protests, recruiting measures became more realistic and less objectionable. However, every so often, violations are uncovered and colleges are penalized by the N.C.A.A.

2. *There are many who feel that the role of sports in our society has completely grown out of hand.* There is too much idolization of athletes, too much glamorization of sports events, and, in general, just too much interest in sports to the neglect of cultural and academic pursuits. Although sports have always been accepted as a phase of physical education, physical educators are questioning the validity of such a unity. There are those who feel that big time collegiate sports today are an entirely separate entity from physical education.

3. *Many athletes are spoiled, coddled, overpraised, and glorified.* Their value is overemphasized to society and to themselves. When they are through playing, what contributions will they be able to make to society without their footballs and basketballs? Will they be able to step down from their pedestal and accept a life of reality?

4. *Too much time is taken for athletics and not enough for academic pursuits.* Athletes receive a very narrow education. The time spent for practice and actual contests leaves little for other endeavors. In addition to this time, the emotional tone of sports is such as to affect individuals for a certain period preceding and following the events. Players invariably think about the contests. They become psychologically prepared for them, and afterwards, reflect on important aspects and situations, replay them mentally, with a result that the dreamed outcome is better than the actual one. This situation will also detract from the attention needed for academic work.

5. *Lastly, America has become a country known for its spectators.* The emphasis on sports elevates a few to the sacrifice of many. The onlookers receive a vicarious thrill from watching others perform: they do not express or develop themselves physically or mentally. Varsity teams

control the usage of the best equipment and facilities while the general student body is either allowed to find time before and after practice (usually inconvenient times) or is not permitted at all to use the same equipment and facilities.

PERSONAL REFLECTION ON THE CONTROVERSY

The pros and cons of sport can be debated forever and more can be added to the list proposed above. Contributions of sport potentially counter balance by far its liabilities. Educated, dedicated, and interested coaches have the final say in the benefits sport may offer to all concerned. Communication with the athletes, student body, faculty, and community is the important thing. The values and ideals of the coach can either elevate the stature of sport or degrade it to such a point that it becomes a Roman spectacle. Coaches primarily create the image. They influence the physical, mental, emotional, and social growth of the boys possibly more than any other individual besides the family.

Some of my feelings on the present status of sport coincide with Huizinga, a German philosopher, who wrote *Homo Ludens: Man the Player*. He believes that play is natural; there is a certain element of play behind war, music, art, and everything created and performed by man. However, he wonders what happened to the play element in sport. Rules and strict control has increased, enjoyment for the participants has decreased, and sport has changed to become a business.

I, too, wonder where the play and fun element has gone in sport. Too much emphasis, too much control, too much leadership, too much attention — where can sport go from here?

CONCLUSION

Once again the burden of solution rests on the shoulders of the coach. He can return these elements to sport. He is responsible for and capable of presenting sport to the players and spectators in a manner socially desirable, within proper perspective, and in such a manner that the value of sport is unquestioned. He should not allow pressure to be cast on him by individuals who have no concern for the welfare of the athlete but only to increase the economic and public status of the school. Above all, the coach's ethics and intentions should be such that he is beyond reproach.

Competition, cooperation, enjoyment, mind and body development, — these are the major potential contributions of sport to the participant. *Are you, the coach, considerate of these factors or is your only concern winning?*

---

3 ENVIRONMENTAL FACTORS OF CHILDHOOD COMPETITIVE ATHLETICS*

By Linus J. Dowell**

The desirability of highly organized athletics for boys below the ninth grade has become a major controversial issue. Elementary schools have for many years felt pressure to adopt the characteristics of interscholastic athletics. The problem has just recently been brought into focus by the wide spread of Little League Baseball throughout the nation.

In order to gain insight into problems of competition for the 15 and under boy, one need only to look at the pro's and con's of athletics for this age group. It is indeed important for parents to understand the strengths and weaknesses of athletics for youngsters so that they may develop ways to improve on the good points and eliminate those practices that are undesirable.

A search through the literature shows a lack of agreement exists between educators, coaches, child specialists and sportswriters in regard to policies and practices, advantages, and dis-

*From The Physical Educator **28**:17-20, March 1971.
**Dr. Dowell, a long time contributor, is a professor at Texas A & M, College Station.

advantages of such participation in competitive athletics. There are however, many points which are held by several authors and attract attention. A summary of the feelings and research findings favoring competitive participation for the 15 and under child are listed in the following paragraphs.

FACTORS SUPPORTING BOYS UNDER 15 PARTICIPATING IN COMPETITIVE ATHLETICS
Physical benefits

a. The sedentary habits of living associated with our highly mechanized society creates an urgent need for increasing the opportunities for all students to participate in vigorous physical abilities. (59)
b. Boys participating in Little Leagues of championship caliber are biologically advanced. This is a positive factor in young boys participating in competitive sports. (33)
c. Boys are naturally physically active and need physical activity. (46)
d. Competitive athletics satisfies the need for physical activity at this age. (61)
e. Boys who participate in athletics show greater motor ability than boys who do not participate. (56)
f. Boys who participate in competitive sports are more mature, and more highly skilled than boys who have no experience in competitive organizations and leagues. (19)
g. Although two physicians interpreted high heart rates associated with basketball to be a possible strain on the circulatory system, scientific evidence indicates that a normal heart cannot be injured by strenuous physical activity. (18)
h. Children of this age need "vigorous physical activity to promote normal growth and development." To satisfy their organic needs and desires, they must have strenuous physical activity in the form of competitive sports. They need adventure and violent physical exertion. (24)
i. Today's children are taller, heavier and more mature than their predecessors. The average weight and height of our population found in children at the age of pubescence or just preceding pubescence indicates an advancement in the rate of maturation. Thus, when adults think of the maturity of a sixth-grader, they must not think of how sixth-graders behaved when they were children. If interscholastic athletics were acceptable for high school students 30 years ago, then they are now acceptable for junior high school boys, and what they did 30 years ago can now be done by boys two years younger. (20)

Emotional benefits

a. Children learn to escape from emotional upsets by physical self-expression in sports. (34)
b. Individual guidance, relaxation and proper diet can

help emotionalism, depending on how intense the case is in the beginner. (26)
c. Competitive sports aids children in becoming emotionally stable. (61)
d. Children get just as emotional over music solos and dramatic performances as over competitive athletics. They cry when they fail spelling tests, yet we do not separate them from spelling. (5)
e. Information about emotion derived from a galvanic skin response test supports the conclusion that Little-League-type competition is no more stimulating than competition in school physical education. (55)
f. Athletics, which tap most of the emotions, can help the real adolescent learn to control himself. This is a very real and positive contribution to the education of the child. (29)

Social benefits

a. Sports can be used as a powerful tool in teaching habits, attitudes, and characteristics of good citizenship. (40)
b. Boys who participate in athletics are better adjusted socially and better adjusted emotionally than boys who do not participate. (56)
c. Boys who participate in competitive sports are more socially accepted, better adjusted and have broader interest than boys who have no experiences in competitive organizations and leagues. (19)
d. Competitive athletics provides an environment that is socially desirable for the pre-teen age child. (32)
e. Athletics provide a setting for good social experience. (46)

Competitive benefits

a. Children are ready to learn games, sports skills and for participation in competitive athletics. (23)
b. All youths have the desire to participate in competitive games. (49)
c. Athletics must not be extinguished nor permitted to go to extremes, but must be properly controlled at the elementary level for there is going to be a certain amount of competitive activity. (21)
d. Schools should prepare the child for competition. (8)
e. Youth feel the need to compete in strenuous athletic games. (2)
f. Children have a desire to play other schools, to show their school spirit. They want to face an unknown quality occasionally, which perhaps is the reason that youth of other days put to sea or headed west. (62)

Other benefits

a. Organized city wide athletic competitive sports in the upper elementary school grades will go far toward reducing delinquency and putting a premium on physical and emotional fitness. (61)
b. Athletic competition for boys brings about improved

sportmanship, brings about worthy use of leisure time, and is an integrative factor in the community. (46)

c. Boys who participate in athletics show greater achievement in school subjects than those boys who do not participate. (56)

d. The majority of parents whose boys play league baseball and many recreation departments throughout the country approve Little League Baseball for boys. (52)

e. Present practice supports the case for competition at this level. A rather comprehensive survey of junior high schools, made in 1958, reports that over 85 per cent had interscholastic athletic programs and that these programs were supported by 78 per cent of the principals of the schools. (60)

Summary

Those who favor competitive athletics for the 15 and under boy contend that:

1. The movement was born out of the needs and desires of young boys.
2. Here is a chance for youth to enjoy the right to play—one of the greatest heritages of youth.
3. It brings opportunities to learn new games and the improvement of playing skills.
4. There is a tremendous possibility for youngsters to develop personal security and emotional stability.
5. Children who participate in competitive athletics exhibit greater popularity, social esteem and personal and social adjustment.
6. It offers an opportunity to make real friendships with squad members and an opportunity to widen a circle of friends by acquaintance with members of opposing teams and to visit and play in other schools.
7. Children who participate in competitive athletics do better scholastically.
8. It develops physical vigor and desirable habits in health, sanitation, and skills.
9. It presents a chance to observe and exemplify good sportmanship.
10. There is a realization that athletic competition is a privilege that carries definite responsibilities with it.
11. There is a chance to learn that violation of a rule of the game brings a penalty—and that this same sequence follows in the game of life.
12. The gymnasium, playground, and athletic field should be laboratories for testing and improving the activities in the athletic and recreation programs.
13. Athletics exist to keep alive the fun-spirit of youth; to provide a vigorous type of recreation in which abide pleasure, happiness, and joy; to prolong the playtime of youth and preserve the joyous zest for living.
14. Athletics exist to contribute to a healthier type of citizen, the building of sound bodies, the disciplining of character, development of personality and leadership, and the stabilizing of emotional control.

A review of selected articles will acquaint parents with some of the criticism and problems of childhood athletics, to the end that they may recognize problems early so that many of the problems may be alleviated before they become overbearing.

FACTORS AGAINST BOYS UNDER 15 PARTICIPATING IN COMPETITIVE ATHLETICS
Overemphasis on winning

a. Objectives for the pre-teen age youngster in athletics should be fun, participation for all, and less emphasis on winning. (41) (4)

b. Too often the only object of the game is to win. This over-emphasis on winning puts too much pressure on the young athlete. (46)

c. Fait indicates that there are more accident possibilities in interscholastic sports which is perhaps due to additional importance on winning. (17)

d. Athletic competition among children produces strong emotional reactions in adults—parents, teachers, leaders, coaches, and even spectators. These reactions in the adults such as undue stress on "winning the game," undue adulation of the skilled athlete, coercion of the child beyond his ability or interests, all of these may be reflected in children. (51)

e. Sports should be played for the good of the individual rather than the winning or losing. (10) (43)

Physical body underdeveloped

a. The largest three needs of a child are food, sleep, and exercise. Parents usually take care of the first two needs but certain checks should also be put on youngsters to see that they get enough and see that they do not get too much exercise. Bones, muscles and other vital organs are not developed well and need supervision. (11)

b. The physical body is not developed to the extent of participating in athletic competition. (27) (35)

c. Quotes by Dr. C. L. Lowman have read that competitive activity before high school age is highly dangerous because neither skeletal growth, cartilages or joints, not to mention muscles, are sufficiently developed. (3)

d. Children's muscles, tissues, and other vital elements are not ready for the extreme play which goes with competition. Sometimes chronic fatigue and other dangerous deterrents enter into these small bodies and the analysis is hindering to normal growth. (63)

e. "Competitive sports for all those under age 13 are not desirable" says Dr. John Reichert. Bones and joints lack the normal protection, and violent exercise can overload internal organs and cause trouble. (50)

f. Contact sports should definitely be out for the pre-teen ager. (44)

Emotional strain

a. Competitive athletics tend to develop tensions to a level that is undesirable in the pre-teen age group. (46) (6) (16) (25) (58)
b. Stresses and strains put on children before they are ready lead to extreme cases of emotionalism. (26)
c. An extreme example may be cited that when in a Little League playoff, 'Little Leaguers' cried like babies, wrecked the hotel lobby they stayed in, had no appetite, had upset stomachs, and some could not even sleep. (3)

Need for maturation

a. Success depends on maturation. A boy with wide experience in a variety of fundamentals will become the superior athlete. These wide experiences are not found in athletics for the youngster. (36) (39) (42)
b. Children are too immature to participate in competitive athletics where pressure is applied by adults, overemphasis on winning, and long trips out of town are the rule rather than the exception. (28) (31) (48)
c. Starting complex team activities or difficult skills at a grade level when children are not sufficiently mature and lack ability to attain success, is a deterrent to the development of athletic ability in most children. This is especially true of the slow maturers who are the ones who will grow into the largest adults and potentially the best athletes in many of our most popular games. (15) (47)

Only a few sports selected

a. With over 54 sports to choose from we end up in school with four main ones. This tends to make a spectator out of the many and players out of the few. (28)
b. Elementary school children should be developing skills and interests in a great variety of activities. Their participation should be broad in nature, rather than specialized. (1) (13)
c. Activities should be varied to give a well developed whole child. (10)
d. They should learn balance, flexibility, agility, coordination, etc. and all boys should play in lead-up games not just only in a few sports which is usually the case in league competition. (42) (54)

Adults run the leagues

a. The only thing wrong with leagues for children is the adults who run the leagues. (28)
b. Adult leadership determines the length of practice and play periods, and resultant pressure can cause the boys to play too long. (12)
c. Boys tend to participate to a fatigue level when egged on by social pressures from adults. (61)
d. For a good program, adults must put emphasis on games for fun instead of games to win. (43)
e. The program can be controlled to the extent that the entertainment features of the program do not detract from its educational aspects. Primary emphasis should be placed on providing educational experience for the participant rather than producing a winning team or providing entertainment for mother, father, and relatives. (59)

Other criticisms

a. Physical fitness for all students should be the major objective of athletics for the pre-teenager rather than competitive sports for the few. (57)
b. Many youngsters participate in all practices and yet are denied the right to play during the games. (46)
c. Athletic competition causes improper diet, loss of appetite, and upset stomach in youngsters. (3)
d. Because of his age the junior high school boy is likely to be sensitive to the pressure which seems always to prevail in all types of interscholastic competition. (3)
e. Athletic league sponsors do not obtain adequate leadership and sometimes stars develop superior attitudes, and a distorted sense of values. (46)
f. The majority of elementary school teachers are women, and are not prepared to teach the activities. "Women are seldom able to inspire confidence on the part of upper—grade boys through demonstration of kicking, throwing, catching, and in general playing the games of touch football, basketball, or softball." (22)

Comments

a. To make a responsible adult, our childhood depends on wholesome competition. The question is the level and intensity of participation at various levels of development. (50)
b. Palmer in study of the effects and values of Little League Baseball on Elementary School boys while in a school environment could draw no conclusions. (45)
c. Seymour found no significant difference in the behavior characteristics of participants and non-participants in Little League. (53)
d. The alternative to organized competition on the elementary school level has been unsupervised "sandlot" competition which, according to Esslinger, "Doctors regard . . . as extremely dangerous." (14)
e. In the final analysis, regardless of the information accumulated, competitive athletics still have to be justified or disqualified on the basis of your individual education programs.
f. Rather than taking the negative approach and spending all their efforts in trying to eliminate competition, school administrators and physical educators should lend their services to help improve and broaden these programs, for the type of competition exemplified by Little League Baseball is here to stay. (38)
g. Midland Texas Public Schools constructed a program for children in grades 4, 5, and 6 which would take pressure off people in the town to develop organized leagues for competition. Emphasis was on

the following three areas: (1) Participation for everyone, (2) Skill development in children and (3) Chance to learn sportsmanship, team play, and competition under more relaxed conditions, than leagues emphasizing winning could afford.

Summary

Those who are against athletic competition for the 15 and under boy contend that:

1. Intense competition is not only educationally unsound, but also detrimental to the physical, psychological, and emotional well-being of young boys.
2. A broad, well-rounded intramural-type program would better serve the needs of boys than an interschool type program.
3. Many players are disturbed because they are not given a chance to play in games even though they came out regularly for practices.
4. Those in charge of the program should be more selective in the recruitment of officials, managers, and coaches.
5. The majority of boys devote from half to most of their leisure time throughout the year in the one interschool sport.
6. Sleeping and eating habits of many of the boys are disturbed for organized competitive sports.
7. Many of the participants on the athletic teams are not ready for organized competitive sports.
8. Poor form and techniques are developed because of insufficient strength and size to perform the skills required.
9. Trips are socially undesirable for this age group.

Before school children are permitted to participate in interschool athletic contests, play days, sports days sponsored by local schools, or similar competition sponsored by nonschool groups, parents should try to see that the following guidelines are adhered to.

GUIDELINES

1. Equate young children on teams according to maturation level.
2. Select activities appropriate to the age and developmental level of players.
3. Require medical examinations before participation, medical supervision during games, and provide minimum accident insurance.
4. Provide competition only on a school, neighborhood or community level.
5. Insure reasonable schedules in terms of frequency and time of day of contests.
6. Modify athletic games to match the maturation level of participants, e.g., smaller balls, smaller playing area, lower goals, shorter distances, shorter times, etc.
7. Change the rules of the game so that every boy on each team can play at least a short time in every game.
8. Provide shorter training seasons, shorter tournament play and encourage players to participate in a variety of activities.
9. Participation in league play should be on a voluntary basis without undue emphasis on any special programs or sport.
10. Do not participate in state, regional, and national tournaments, bowl, charity, or exhibition games with children 12 years of age and under.
11. Be especially careful of contact sports; use tennis shoes, proper equipment, pads, helmet, etc.
12. In order to insure an adequate program for children of this age group, alert the community to the need for personnel, facilities, equipment, and supplies.
13. Professional leaders who are well qualified must act as coaches.
14. See that coaches:
    A. Learn the rules of the game.
    B. Conduct training programs for managers and officials and attend a workshop with other coaches to improve skills.
    C. Coach boys for the fun of coaching, for the fun of playing, to the end that they will build strong bodies, discipline character, develop personality and leadership and help to stabilize emotions.
    D. Beware of commercial exploitation of players.
    E. Treat players as individual developing personalities.
    F. Are observant to injury, respond to fatigue, and the emotional needs of players.
    G. Encourage less emphasis on winning, fewer spectators, less pressure from parents, and less publicity and promotion in order to reduce tensions in your players.
    H. Exemplify good sportsmanship; respect referee's decisions, etc., and see that spectators and players do also.

And last but by no means least, carry on a continuous public relations program to educate the community, and especially the parents to these guidelines and to good sportsmanship.

BIBLIOGRAPHY

1. Anderson, John E., "Present Levels of Understanding Regarding Child Growth and Development," *American Academy of Physical Education, Professional Contributions,* 6:8, 1958.
2. "Are Little Leagues Good for Youngsters," *Science Digest,* 40:49, November, 1956.
3. "Athletic Competition for Children," *Athletic Journal,* 34:18, January, 1954.
4. Attaway, J., "Athletics and the Elementary School," *Texas Outlook,* 49:30-31, November, 1965.
5. Bradshaw, James, "Re: Highly Organized Sports for Small Boys? . . . A Debate," *The Rotarian,* 93:49, October, 1958.

6. Bucher, Charles A., "Little League Can Hurt Your Boy," *Look,* 18:3, September 22, 1953.

7. Chapman, G. R., "After-School Recreation for Elementary Children," *Journal of Health, Physical Education, and Recreation,* 26:14-15, November, 1955.

8. "Competition for Children: Theory versus Practice," *Athletic Journal,* 39:32, January, 1959.

9. "Competitive Sports Hold Peril for Pre-Teenagers," *Science Digest,* 44:50, November, 1958.

10. "Desirable Athletic Competition for Children," *Journal of Health, Physical Education, and Recreation,* 23:21-22, June, 1952.

11. "Don't Rush Your Child into Athletics," *Science Digest,* 34:53-57, September, 1953.

12. Dukelow, D. A., and F. V. Hein, "Junior High Athletic Leagues," *Today's Health,* 29:13, November, 1951.

13. Dukelow, Donald A., "A Doctor Looks at Exercise and Fitness," *Journal of Health, Physical Education, and Recreation,* 28:26, September, 1957.

14. Esslinger, Arthur, "Out-of-School Athletics for Children," *American Academy of Physical Education, Professional Contributions,* 3:39, November, 1954.

15. Evans, W. R., "Developing Athletic Ability," *National Elementary Principal,* 39:17-20, April, 1960.

16. Fait, Hollis, "An Analytical Study of the Effects of Competitive Athletics Upon Junior High School Boys," Unpublished dissertation, University of Iowa, August, 1961.

17. Fait, Hollis F., "Should the Junior High School Sponsor Interscholastic Athletic Competition?" *Journal of Health, Physical Education, and Recreation,* 32:21, February, 1961.

18. Hale, Creighton J., "Athletic Competition for Children," *Athletic Journal,* 34:190-192, January, 1954.

19. Hale, Creighton J., "Athletics for Pre-High School Age Children," *Journal of Health, Physical Education, and Recreation,* 30:19-21, December, 1959.

20. Hale, Creighton J., "Changing Growth Patterns of the American Child," *Education,* 78:468, April, 1958.

21. Hanson, E. H., "Athletic for Children," *American School Board Journal,* 128-31, June, 1954.

22. Henderson, Edwin B., "An Experiment in Elementary School Athletics," *Journal of Health, Physical Education, and Recreation,* 22:21, June, 1951.

23. Hess, L. A., "Competitive Athletics for my Son," *Childhood Education,* 31:441-442, May, 1955.

24. "Is This a Sensible Junior High Interscholastic Athletic Code," *Ohio High School Athlete,* 17:126, April, 1958.

25. Jersild, A. T. and H. E. Jones, "Adolescent Growth Study," *Journal of Consulting Psychology,* 3:157-159, 1939.

26. Johnson, W. R., "Emotional Upset in the Athlete," *Athletic Journal,* 32:16, November, 1951.

27. Keene, C. H., "Sports and Games in the School Schedule," *Hygeia,* 20:557-558, July, 1942.

28. "Kids and Athletics," *Changing Times,* 15:22-24, October, 1961.

29. "Kid Emotions," *Athletic Journal,* 40:20, March, 1960.

30. Kleinman, S., "School Athletics—An Analysis," *Ohio High School Athlete,* 17:101, February, 1958.

31. Knapp, C. and H. Combes, "Does Basketball Belong in Grade School," *Athletic Journal,* 30:51-52, January, 1950.

32. Koss, R. S., "Guidelines for the Improvement of Physical Education in Selected Public Elementary Schools in New Jersey," *Research Quarterly,* 36:282-288, October, 1965.

33. Krogman, W. M., "Maturation Age of Fifty-five Boys in the Little League World Series," *Research Quarterly,* 30:54-56.

34. Lawther, J. D., "Role of the Coach in American Education," *Journal of Health, Physical Education, and Recreation,* 36:65-66, May, 1965.

35. Lowman, C. L., "A Consideration of Teen-Age Athletics," *Journal of Health, Physical Education, and Recreation,* 12:398-399, September, 1941.

36. Marett, L., "Fit Sports for Pre-Teens," *Parents Magazine,* 38:54-55, June, 1963.

37. McCracken, Oliver, Jr., "Do Interscholastic Athletics in The Junior School Aid or Retard a Desirable Educational Program?", *Bulletin of National Association of Secondary School Principals,* 44:99-100, April, 1960.

38. McCraw, Lynn W., "Athletics and Elementary School Children," *Texas Outlook,* 39:13, June, 1955.

39. McNeely, S. A., "What Kind of Athletics for Children," *National Elementary Principal,* 32:28-29, October, 1952.

40. Miller, K. D., "Children's Sports," *Today's Health,* 35:18-20, May, 1957.

41. Miller, R. D., "Elementary School Activities," *School Activities,* 32:245-246, April, 1961.

42. Morris, M., "Don't Rush Your Kids," *Journal of Health, Physical Education, and Recreation,* 23:18-19, October, 1952.

43. Murphy, A. C., "How Can We Live with Competition," *Childhood Education,* 31:439-441, May, 1955.

44. "No Football for Pre-Teens," *Science News Letter,* 70:216, October 6, 1956.

45. Palmer, James J., "A Critical Evaluation by Teachers of the Effects and Values of 'Little League Baseball' on Elementary School Boys While in a School Environment," Unpublished Master's Thesis, Boston University, 1956.

46. Patterson, N. A., "Are Little Leaguers too Big for their Britches," *Childhood Education,* 35:359-361, April, 1959.

47. Powers, L. H., "Changing Perspective Regarding After-School Sports," *School Activities,* 32:201-209, March, 1961.

48. "Recommendations from the Seattle Convention Workshops," *Journal of Health, Physical Education, and Recreation,* 18:432, September, 1947.

49. Rehange, K. J. and S. J. Heywood, "Athletic Competition for Children," *Elementary School Journal,* 53:375-377, March, 1953.

50. Reichert, J. L., "Pediatricians View of Competitive Sports Before the Teens," *Today's Health,* 35:28-31, October, 1957.

51. Report, Committee on School Health, "Competitive Athletics," *Pediatrics,* 18:674, October, 1956.

52. Scott, Phebe, "Attitudes Toward Athletic Competition in Elementary Schools," *Research Quarterly,* 24:352-361, October, 1953.

53. Seymour, Emery W., "A Comparative Study of Certain Behavior Characteristic of Participant and Non-Participation Boys in Little League Baseball," Unpublished Master's Thesis, Springfield College, 1955.

54. Shaw, John H., "Standards for Junior High School Athletics," *Journal of School Health,* 34:164-168, April, 1964.

55. Skubic, Elvera, "Emotional Responses of Boys to Little League and Middle League Competitive Baseball," *Research Quarterly,* 26:342-352, October, 1955.

56. Skubic, Elvera, "Studies of Little League and Middle League Baseball," *Research Quarterly,* 27:97-110, March, 1956.

57. "Soft Pedal the Accent on Sports," *Nations Schools,* 74:57, November, 1964.

58. Solomon, Ben, "Little League—Menace or Blessing? *Youth Leaders Digest,* 15:161-213, February, 1953.

59. "Standards for Junior High School Athletics," Washington, D. C., American Association for Health, Physical Education, and Recreation, 1963, p. 11.

60. Tompkins, Ellsworth, and Virginia Roe, "A Survey of Interscholastic Athletic Programs in Separately Organized Junior High Schools," *Bulletin of National Association of Secondary School Principals,* 42:1-47, November, 1958.

61. "Wartime Activity for Pre-Adolescent Boys," *Journal of Health, Physical Education, and Recreation,* 16:17, January, 1945.

62. Werner, George I., "Interscholastic Athletics," *Journal of Health, Physical Education, and Recreation,* 19:467, September, 1948.

63. "What About Organized Competitive Sports for Children," *Safety Education,* 36:35-37, October, 1956.

64. "What Kind of Athletics for Children," *Education Digest,* 18:43-45, December, 1952.

4 WOMEN'S ATHLETICS—WHAT IS OUR FUTURE?*

By Lou Jean Moyer
A member of the Physical Education Department at Northern Illinois University, DeKalb, Illinois 60115. This article is adapted from a speech presented at the Northwest District AAHPER Convention in April 1976.

At this stage of our development, everyone is asking, "What is the future of women's athletics?" Television coverage of women's athletic events, magazine feature articles, and newspaper stories are doing much to inform the public about the accomplishments of these young women. The stereotyped view of the female athlete is becoming clouded as women athletes are charming and gaining the respect of their countryfolk. So where is women's sport headed? Probably toward professionalism, toward excesses, and toward acceptance by our society as a worthy activity for women. We, as educators, will like some aspects and dislike others, but women *will* participate, get

*From The Journal of Physical Education and Recreation **48:**52, 54, January 1977.

recognition, and enjoy the freedom of sport participation more than ever before in the history of our country.

This change has been gaining momentum for years and has exploded into reality during the last two years. Capitol Hill has been bombarded with reactions to the Title IX regulations—the Tower Amendment and later the Tower Bill, the Casey Amendment, the Helms Bill, the O'Hara Bill, and more recently the declaratory complaint filed by the NCAA against the Office of Health, Education and Welfare. All have been attempts to weaken or eradicate the regulations as they affect athletic opportunities for girls and women in schools. The implications of these efforts and their influence greatly affect the future of teaching physical education as well as the development of interscholastic and intercollegiate athletics for both sexes. The current slashing of school budgets and elimination of programs is a further development which has put us on the defensive, but even if Title IX ceased to exist administrators could do little to hold back the move in educational institutions toward equal opportunity in sport for women. The surge has gained momentum and expanded women's programs will be demanded by students and parents.

Whether one supports the language in the Title IX regulations or is in sympathy with big time athletics, it seems that somewhere between Congress, the NCAA, and the female lobbyists, the educational interests of the participants have been lost. The intent of Title IX was to give all students and employees of federally funded institutions equal opportunity. In practice, the implementation rather than the outcome has become the issue as people work to protect the financial interests of big time athletics.

ATHLETICS—ENTERTAINMENT OR EDUCATION?

Is athletics, as offered in school, merely a commodity to be exploited, or is it an educational program deserving educational funding? If an activity deserves a place in any school curriculum it must be planned, implemented, and evaluated by educational values for the student or participant, in light of the basic philosophy of education and of the specific school. Should athletics be a part of the total school curriculum? If it is an educational program, it should be treated like any other educational program using educational criteria for its implementation and evaluation. Before a program can be evaluated, however, a philosophy must be established so the leaders of the program will understand what is expected of them. What is the philosophical position of athletics in individual schools? Is the objective of the athletic program to become the state champion? To enrich the life of the participant? To entertain the community? Does each school have a philosophy? Who makes the school philosophical position? Is the philosophy practical? Does it reflect educational goals? Is the philosophy consistent with practices? Has it been established to reflect boys and girls programs? Have those in leadership positions in the boys and girls programs contributed equally to the establishment of these purposes? Are we trying to rid athletics of abuses?

It seems that school administrators, the leaders of physical education and school athletics, men and women alike in a given school or school district need to sit down together to examine present programs and determine the athletic philosophy of their school. The time for planning is now. HEW tells us there must be change to effect equal opportunity by June 1978. So we need to plan for it and develop our programs in light of it rather than let the change manipulate our objectives. The planning and changing will affect both the women's and the men's programs so women cannot ignore the concerns of the men in the push for equal opportunity. It is not the men's fault that for many years women physical educators did not want athletic programs for girls and women when the men were developing their programs. What objectives do we seek in a program of athletics? What is their order of priority and what steps must we take to reach them?

First we must determine the philosophy and purpose of the athletic program. If the purpose is entertainment, then it is obvious the program should be planned with the values of the spectator in mind. Athletics, then, would not be for the education of the participant and should be treated as a business enterprise. Athletes would become professionals working to serve their audience. The management must be concerned with producing enough income to support it, getting a coach clever enough about the game to win in most close contests, planning the program to get the most out of the participants, establishing a building program to assure continual high quality teams, and attracting athletes from a variety of geographical areas necessary for this building program. Many big time university athletic programs, especially in football and basketball, already have these objectives as their primary goal. In the name of Title IX, is this what will happen to women's programs?

If athletic programs are to be for the participants and truly are to be expanded educational programs, then they must be planned, executed, and evaluated with *educational* objectives in mind. The questions which must be answered are: Are the participants learning about themselves as individuals? Are the athletes learning to recognize and appreciate excellent performance in teammates and in opponents? Are the students reflecting the values of sportsmanship and fair play in their everyday existence? Do the athletes understand, participate in making, and abide by the policies and regulations of training and conditioning? The list goes on. Because we, as educators, have not been able to decide what place athletics rightfully has in an educational setting, we have not been able to evaluate it objectively. We see it as all things to all people—an educational experience for young people, a vital link with the taxpayer in public relations, and entertainment for the school and community. I propose that one cannot create a good program for one group without shortchanging the others; therefore, it appears that we are on a merry-go-round repeating mistakes over and over, justifying our actions in terms of the situation rather than of the principle or value involved. We begin with an educational program for the participants until a coach, principal, or administrator ignores a minor rule infraction to acquire the winning edge.

We have difficulty determining what is right and what is wrong because practice has made wrong seem right. We *must* develop a sound philosophy of athletics in education and then see that our actions mirror our philosophy.

WHO SHOULD LEAD?

Second, we must determine who will lead the program in light of the values sought. Traditionally, it has been the physical education teacher who has given leadership to the limited girls and women's athletic programs. Because the variety and length of season was minimal and an outgrowth of physical education classes, this plan of administration worked. Because of the physical education backgrounds of these women, we had leadership which demanded fair play and sought educational goals, and we had administrators who cared little about past won-lost records. There were few tournaments which culminated in a championship; therefore there was little pressure from the public, and we were content with our motto, "a sport for every girl and a girl in every sport."

Traditionally, those in leadership positions for boys and men's programs were those who had participated in intercollegiate athletics and were themselves successful players, or players for a successful coach. Selection of personnel for an athletic program of a high school or college was based on the probability of the coach's success as measured by the won-lost record. Some of these coaches were physical educators in the truest sense of the word in that the participants were more important to them than the record; however, since school administrators seemed to place a value on the success of the boys teams

as recorded in the won-lost columns of the season, physical educators were often relieved of coaching responsibilities or quit coaching voluntarily because the administration's expectations were in opposition to the coach's personal objectives in an athletic program. If the coach wished to retain his job, he had to produce a winning team.

Who will be the leaders of women's athletic programs now? Can the leadership avoid the pressures of the need to win at all costs? Will the outcome be more important than the process? When the value of the outcome exceeds the value of the process, the educational objectives of the athletic program are in danger and the place of an athletic program in school is in serious jeopardy. We can assure quality leadership only by selecting competent coaches who believe that personal values are more important than the team record.

WHICH VALUES ARE IMPORTANT?

In the area of values to the participant, we have been quite remiss in planning and evaluating the total program of athletics, for the value seems to have been measured by the won-lost record. Is that what women want in athletics in the name of equality of opportunity? It is easy to divide and equate money, facilities, time, and equipment, but the intangible values learned through athletic experiences are much more difficult to measure. Yet, in my opinion, the values learned represent the most important aspect of athletics. There are social, intellectual, moral, and ethical values to be gained through a program of athletics, and in no other aspect of school does a better opportunity exist to teach the values reflected in many of these areas. These moral and ethical values, when applied, make up the substance of an individual and must receive high priority. Equal funding for boys and girls does not elicit high moral and ethical values from the recipients. Equal use of facilities does not effect intellectual values. Equal opportunity does not force productive social values, but the values that the participant gains from competition can be measured by the quality of the life of the participant. These qualities will be measurable human traits long after the won-lost records have been forgotten.

For years some have justified a sports program in schools by citing the values which accrue to the participant, as if being involved would automatically enhance self-esteem based on the standard of fair play, good sportsmanship, and respect and consideration of others. If these values are adopted it is not inherent in participation but because of the leadership. Leaders alone determine quality athletic programs and establish value systems which reflect educational goals. These emerge only when the administration places educational goals above a won-lost record.

Do sports provide a feeling of security by giving participants opportunities to belong to a group? Can being on a team automatically indicate achievement? Can one automatically gain recognition and importance by attaining goals through participation? Only if the philosophy creates an atmosphere for the leaders to nurture these opportunities. Sports will provide suitable outlets for creative, cooperative, competitive, and aggressive behaviors if the leadership encourages it. Sport can provide cooperation and competition while teaching unity and courage if it is nurtured by the leadership. Yes, sport provides opportunities for value judgments, self-appraisal, and acceptance of personal strengths and weaknesses; however, it is the leader who uses the right moment, the right example, the right tone and inflection who creates these values in athletes. The leaders must place school athletics in their true perspective, be true to educational goals and, most of all, be true to the participant. In this way, there is educational value in sport.

Change is inevitable. We are witnessing change in athletics in the thrust of programs for girls and women. Concurrently, the men's and boys' coaches are showing a possessive attitude toward athletics—a human trait which emerges when one's position is threatened. But is the objective of getting students to enjoy the values of athletics threatened or challenged? It doesn't appear to me that it is. The threat appears to be directed against the excesses.

Women physical educators and coaches are presently enjoying equality in sport stimulated by Title IX and the women's movement, but soon these pleasures will become headaches as some are finding already. Women are finding out what the men have known for years: you cannot have athletics without pressures from parents, administration, and friends; it is easier to say you be-

lieve in ethical values than it is to live them; it is easy to say that values to the participant are more important than winning until you lose to a team that does not have the quality of your team.

FIGHT FOR CHANGE

Where are women's sports headed? Where will we be in 1978 when Title IX is to be fully implemented? Will we, along with the men, be more deeply mired in a program of athletics which does not place educational values high on the list of priorities? I am encouraged by the strong interest college presidents are beginning to take in the NCAA and in shaping the athletic programs on their campuses. It appears their organized effort has stemmed from a concern over violations as well as the financing of expanded programs. Maybe this is really a blessing in disguise, for the principles and objectives of intercollegiate athletics will surely now be evaluated. We can begin to bring sanity back to athletics through a revitalized inspection of values, but physical educators must *participate!*

Fight for the educational goals of an athletic program. I am convinced that a majority of men coaches are ready for a change. They just don't want to be the *first* to capitulate, so these changes must occur in conferences and ultimately in the national organizations. Those in leadership roles of the high school programs are also going to have to do some serious evaluating and planning. We cannot continue to have a girls bowling team dominated by boys as was the situation in Illinois in 1975, nor can we allow a boy on a girls volleyball team to intimidate the girls on the opposite team as occurred in the Indiana State Girls Volleyball Championship in 1976. Equal opportunity in sport for both boys and girls is needed. We must see that it occurs.

There are disquieting times ahead. Change is always a time to ponder, but let's not ponder so long about values and objectives and be so afraid to take a stand that we all become spectators in the contest of growing opportunities for women vs. the economic pinch while the current values, mixed up and ill-defined purposes, and philosophies dictate how athletic programs will be operated. We educators have a job to do. Let's do it!

SUPPLEMENTAL READINGS
Objectives of competitive athletics
1930-1939

5. Abernethy, R. R.: A sane athletic program, The Journal of Health and Physical Education 7:133-135, 207, March 1936.
6. Moench, F. J.: High school athletics in a modern educational program, The Journal of Health and Physical Education 4:30-31, 56-57, December 1933.

1950-1959

7. Calisch, Richard: The sportsmanship myth, The Physical Educator 10:9-11, March 1953.
8. Fait, Hollis F.: Competitive athletics—culprit or contributor in emotional development? The Physical Educator 13:130-131, December 1956.
9. Forsythe, Charles E.: An examination of basic concepts for athletics in the space age, Journal of Health, Physical Education, and Recreation 29:28-30, September 1958.
10. Hughes, William L.: The place of athletics in the school physical-education program, The Journal 21:23-27, December 1950.
11. Mikula, Thomas: Winning isn't all, The Journal of the American Association for Health, Physical Education, and Recreation 24:17, 47, October 1953.

1960-1969

12. Bucher, Charles A.: Needed: a new athletic program, The Physical Educator 23:99-102, October 1966.
13. Division of Men's Athletics of the American Association for Health, Physical Education, and Recreation: Athletics in education, Journal of Health, Physical Education, and Recreation 33:24-27, 59, September 1962.
14. Genasci, James E., and Klissouras, Vasillis: The Delphic spirit in sports, Journal of Health, Physical Education, and Recreation 37:43-45, February 1966.
15. Larson, Leonard A.: Why sports participation? Journal of Health, Physical Education, and Recreation 35:36-37, 42-43, January 1964.
16. Morsink, Helen M.: The "extra" in extra-curricular sports, The Physical Educator 26:59-60, May 1969.
17. Oberteuffer, Delbert: On learning values through sport, Quest 1:23-29, December 1963.

1970-1979

18. Bosco, James S.: Winning at all cost, costs! The Physical Educator 34:35-37, March 1977.
19. Brown, Roscoe C., Jr.: Sport; whose bag? III. Is sport really colorblind? Quest 19:91-92, January 1973.
20. Kleinman, Seymour: Sport; whose bag? IV. Is sport experience? Quest 19:93-96, January 1973.
21. Locke, L. F.: Sport; whose bag? II. Are sports education? Quest 19:87-90, January 1973.
22. Morford, W. R.: Sport; whose bag? I. Is sport the struggle or the triumph? Quest 19:83-86, January 1973.
23. Scott, Jack: Sport and the radical ethic, Quest 19:71-77, January 1973.
24. Shultz, Fredrick D.: Broadening the athletic experience, Journal of Health, Physical Education, and Recreation 43:45-47, April 1972.
25. Snyder, Eldon E., and Spreitzer, Elmer: Basic assumptions in the world of sports, Quest 24:3-9, Summer 1975.
26. Wilkerson, Martha, and Dodder, Richard A.: What does sport do for people? The Journal of Physical Education and Recreation 50:50-51, February 1979.

The relationship between athletics and physical education programs
1930-1939

27. Abernethy, R. R.: A sane athletic program, The Journal of Health and Physical Education 7:133-135, 207, March 1936.
28. Brown, Robert: Interscholastic athletics in the school curriculum, The Jour-

nal of Health and Physical Education **10:**230-232, 256-257, April 1939.

29. La Porte, William Ralph: Is our athletic philosophy sound? The Journal of Health and Physical Education **10:**580-581, 604-605, December 1939.

1940-1949

30. Johnson, Ernest Y.: The place of athletics in the physical education program, The Physical Educator **2:**35-36, October 1941.

31. Langton, Clair V.: The relation of athletics to physical education, The Physical Educator **1:**98-100, February 1941.

1950-1959

32. Falgren, Lloyd H.: School policies to govern administration of interscholastic athletics, The Physical Educator **7:**110-112, December 1950.

33. Hughes, William L.: The place of athletics in the school physical-education program, The Journal **21:**23-27, December 1950.

34. Seidler, A. H.: Athletics and physical education, The Physical Educator **10:**104-105, December 1953.

1960-1969

35. Baley, James A.: Physical education and athletics belong together, The Physical Educator **23:**77-78, May 1966.

Childhood athletics
1930-1939

36. Abernethy, R. R.: A sane athletic program, The Journal of Health and Physical Education **7:**133-135, 207, March 1936.

37. Hussey, Marguerite M.: Adaptation of athletic activity to the elementary school, The Journal of Health and Physical Education **4:**31, 60-61, February 1933.

1940-1949

38. Lowman, C. L.: A consideration of teen age athletics, The Journal of

Health and Physical Education **12:**398-399, September 1941.

39. Lowman, C. L.: The vulnerable age, The Journal of Health and Physical Education **18:**635-636, November 1947.

40. Werner, George I.: Interscholastic athletics, The Journal of Health and Physical Education **19:**466-467, 511-513, September 1948.

1950-1959

41. American Association for Health, Physical Education, and Recreation: Desirable athletics for children, The Journal of the American Association for Health, Physical Education, and Recreation **23:**21-22, June 1952.

42. Hale, Creighton J.: What research says about athletics for pre–high school age children, Journal of Health, Physical Education, and Recreation **30:**19-21, 43, December 1959.

43. Hughes, William L.: The place of athletics in the school physical-education program, The Journal **21:**23-27, December 1950.

44. Knapp, Clyde, and Combes, Harry A.: Elementary interscholastic basketball—does this produce superior high-school players? The Journal of the American Association for Health, Physical Education, and Recreation **24:**12-13, 37, November 1953.

45. McNeely, Simon A.: Of "Mouse" and men, The Journal of the American Association for Health, Physical Education, and Recreation **23:**27-28, December 1952.

1960-1969

46. Fait, Hollis F.: Should the junior high sponsor interscholastic athletic competition? Journal of Health, Physical Education, and Recreation **32:**20-22, February 1961.

47. Frank, James: Elementary school—not too early for interscholastic sports, The Physical Educator **22:**9-11, March 1965.

1970-1979

48. Bucher, Charles A.: Athletic competition and the developmental growth pattern, The Physical Educator **28:**3-4, March 1971.
49. Bula, Michael R.: Competition for children; the real issue, Journal of Health, Physical Education, and Recreation **42:** 40, September 1971.
50. Burke, Edmund J., and Kleiber, Douglas: Psychological and physical implications of highly competitive sports for children, The Physical Educator **33:**63-70, May 1976.
51. Dellastatious, J. W., and Cooper, Walter: The physiological aspects of competitive sports for young athletes, The Physical Educator **27:**3-5, March 1970.
52. Gilliam, Thomas: Fitness through youth sports; myth or reality? The Journal of Physical Education and Recreation **49:** 41-42, March 1978.
53. Mehl, Jack, and Davis, William W.: Youth sports for fun—and whose benefit? The Journal of Physical Education and Recreation **49:**48-49, March 1978.
54. Smoll, Frank L., Smith, Ronald E., and Curtis, Bill: Behavioral guidelines for youth sport coaches, The Journal of Physical Education and Recreation **49:** 46-47, March 1978.
55. Thomas, Jerry R.: Is winning essential to the success of youth sports contests? The Journal of Physical Education and Recreation **49:**42-43, March 1978.

Athletic programs for females
1930-1939

56. Case, Emily I.: Carry over of school athletics, The Journal of Health and Physical Education **8:**550-551, 578-579, November 1937.
57. Daviess, Grace B.: In answer to "Why cramp competition?" The Journal of Health and Physical Education **2:**29, 63, March 1931.
58. Gittings, Ina E.: Why cramp competition? The Journal of Health and Physical Education **2:**10-12, 54, January 1931.

59. Hodgkins, Anne F.: In answer to "Why cramp competition?" The Journal of Health and Physical Education **2:**29, 63, March 1931.
60. Savage, Howard J.: Athletics for women from a national point of view, The Journal of Health and Physical Education **1:**12-16, 42, June 1930.
61. Smith, Helen N.: Evils of sports for women, The Journal of Health and Physical Education **2:**8-9, 50-51, January 1931.

1940-1949

62. National Section on Women's Athletics of the American Association for Health, Physical Education, and Recreation: Desirable practices in athletics for girls and women, The Journal of Health and Physical Education **12:**422, 424, September 1941.

1950-1959

63. Hartman, Betty G.: On intercollegiate competition for women, Journal of Health, Physical Education, and Recreation **29:**24, March 1958.
64. Means, Clarence G.: Let the girls play, too, Journal of Health, Physical Education, and Recreation **29:**22, May-June 1958.

1960-1969

65. Clifton, Marguerite A.: The future of intercollegiate sports for women, The Physical Educator **23:**158-162, December 1966.
66. Coffey, Margaret A.: Then & now; the sportswoman, Journal of Health, Physical Education, and Recreation **36:**38-41, 50, February 1965.
67. Division for Girls and Women's Sports of the American Association for Health, Physical Education, and Recreation: Statement of policies for competition in girls and women's sports, Journal of Health, Physical Education, and Recreation **34:**31-33, September 1963.
68. Division for Girls and Women's Sports

of the American Association for Health, Physical Education, and Recreation: The future of interscholastic sports for girls, Journal of Health, Physical Education, and Recreation **39**:39-41, March 1968.

69. Lambert, Charlotte: Pros and cons of intercollegiate competition for women; a middle of the road position paper, Journal of Health, Physical Education, and Recreation **40**:75, 77-78, May 1969.

70. Stanley, D. K., and Leavitt, Norma, editors: Basic issues, Journal of Health, Physical Education, and Recreation **33**:6, 8, 10, May-June 1962.

1970-1979

71. Arnold, Don E.: Compliance with Title IX in secondary school physical education, The Journal of Physical Education and Recreation **48**:19-22, January 1977. (Refer to Chapter 3.)

72. Corbitt, Richard W., and others: Female athletics; a special communication from the Committee on the Medical Aspects of Sports of the American Medical Association, The Journal of Physical Education and Recreation **46**:45-46, January 1975.

73. Davenport, Joanna: The women's movement into the Olympic Games, The Journal of Physical Education and Recreation **49**:58-60, March 1978.

74. Geadelmann, Patricia L.: Equality in athletics; can separate be equal? The Journal of Physical Education and Recreation **49**:32-33, 72, November-December 1978.

75. Gerber, Ellen W.: The changing female image; a brief commentary on sport competition for women, Journal of Health, Physical Education, and Recreation **42**:59-61, October 1971.

76. Hanson, John F., and Green, Mary L.: The coming of the second plague, The Physical Educator **32**:64-66, May 1975.

77. Harris, Dorothy: Psychological considerations, The Journal of Physical Education and Recreation **46**:32-36, January 1975.

78. Hult, Joan: Separate but equal athletics for women, Journal of Health, Physical Education, and Recreation **44**:57-58, June 1973.

79. Hult, Joan: Competitive athletics for girls—we must act, Journal of Health, Physical Education, and Recreation **45**:45-46, June 1974.

80. Lumpkin, Angela: Let's set the record straight, The Journal of Physical Education and Recreation **48**:40, 42, 44, March 1977.

81. Ryan, Allan J.: Gynecological considerations, The Journal of Physical Education and Recreation **46**:40-44, January 1975.

82. Small, Cathy: Requiem for an issue, Journal of Health, Physical Education, and Recreation **44**:27-28, January 1973.

ASSIGNMENTS
Individual activities

1. Read article 1 and either submit a written report or discuss its implications in class.

2. Submit a paper in which the concept of the development of desirable social traits through competitive athletic experiences is explored.
   ARTICLES: 2, 5, 7, 9, 10, 15-17, 25.

3. Identify and discuss at least five objectives of competitive athletics.
   ARTICLES: 2, 5, 6, 8-10, 12-18, 20-25.

4. Investigate the concept of sport as a model of racial equality.
   ARTICLES: 23-25.

5. Prepare a list of the advantages and disadvantages of both separate and combined administrative organization for athletic and physical education programs.
   ARTICLES: 27-35.

6. Determine the administrative plan (separate or combined) that is more desirable for athletic and physical education programs. Submit a paper defending that plan.
   ARTICLES: 27-35.

7. Prepare a list of pros and cons of orga-

nized competitive athletic experiences during childhood.
ARTICLES: 36-55.

8. Submit a paper examining the effects of program leadership on the outcomes of organized competitive athletic experiences during childhood.
ARTICLES: 45-47, 49-51, 53-55.

9. Examine the evolution of societal attitudes toward the American sportswoman.
ARTICLES: 66, 73, 75, 80.

10. Analyze the competition-for-women controversy of 1931.
ARTICLES: 57-59.

11. List pros and cons of competitive athletics for females.
ARTICLES: 4, 56-61, 63, 64, 69, 70, 72, 77, 81, 82.

12. Prepare a paper examining physiological implications of athletics for females.
ARTICLES: 72, 81.

13. Prepare and defend policies that should be followed in secondary school athletic programs for females.
ARTICLES: 62, 65, 67, 76, 79.

Group presentations

1. Drama
   a. TOPIC: *Justification of interscholastic competitive athletics.*
   b. PARTICIPANTS: Physical educators and coaches representing various time periods; members of a contemporary board of education.
   c. FUNCTIONS: To enact a meeting in which the physical educators and coaches attempt to convince the school board that an interscholastic athletic program should be initiated in the local high school; some of the board members are opposed to such a program.
   d. OBJECTIVES OF PRESENTATION: (1) To identify specific authors and time periods, (2) to present arguments supporting an interscholastic athletic program, (3) to present arguments opposing such a program, (4) to illus-

trate the consistency of opinions throughout the years.
   e. ARTICLES: 2, 5, 6, 8-10, 12-18, 20-25.

2. Drama
   a. TOPIC: *The importance of winning.*
   b. PARTICIPANTS: Physical educators representing various time periods; the athletic director of a local high school.
   c. FUNCTIONS: To enact a meeting in which the athletic director is releasing the head football coach because he has a poor won/lost record; the physical educators attempt to convince the athletic director that competitive athletics involve values and benefits more important than victory or defeat; the athletic director attempts to defend the proposition that a respectable won/lost record is the basis for the coach's employment.
   d. OBJECTIVES OF PRESENTATION: (1) To identify specific authors and time periods, (2) to present arguments identifying desirable outcomes of athletic competition, (3) to present the athletic director's viewpoint that winning is the most important factor, (4) to illustrate the consistency of arguments throughout the years.
   e. ARTICLES: 2, 5, 6, 11, 12, 14, 18, 22, 24.

3. Drama
   a. TOPIC: *Administrative organization for an athletic program.*
   b. PARTICIPANTS: Physical educators from various time periods.
   c. FUNCTIONS: To enact a meeting in which a plan of administrative organization for an athletic program is to be determined.
   d. OBJECTIVES OF PRESENTATION: (1) To identify specific authors and time periods, (2) to present advantages and disadvantages of combined and separate athletic and physical education programs, (3) to determine which administrative plan is more suitable, (4) to illustrate the consis-

tency of arguments throughout the years.

e. ARTICLES: 27-35.

4. Debate

a. TOPIC: *Administrative organization for an athletic program.*

b. PARTICIPANTS: Two teams of three or four students each.

c. FUNCTIONS: To represent physical educators from various time periods.

d. OBJECTIVES OF PRESENTATION: (1) To identify specific authors and time periods, (2) to present advantages and disadvantages of combined and separate athletic and physical education programs, (3) to illustrate the consistency of arguments throughout the years, (4) to convince the class members of the validity of the arguments; class members may vote at the conclusion of the presentation.

e. ARTICLES: 27-35.

5. Debate

a. TOPIC: *Pros and cons of childhood competitive athletics.*

b. PARTICIPANTS: Two teams of three or four students each.

c. FUNCTIONS: To represent physical educators from various time periods.

d. OBJECTIVES OF PRESENTATION: (1) To identify specific authors and time periods, (2) to present arguments supporting organized competitive athletics during childhood, (3) to present arguments opposing organized competitive athletics during childhood, (4) to illustrate the continuing nature of the controversy throughout the years, (5) to convince the class members of the validity of the arguments; class members may vote at the conclusion of the presentation.

e. ARTICLES: 36-55.

6. Drama

a. TOPIC: *Organization and administration of childhood athletic programs.*

b. PARTICIPANTS: Physical educators representing various time periods.

c. FUNCTIONS: To enact a meeting in which an elementary school athletic program is planned and organized.

d. OBJECTIVES OF PRESENTATION: (1) To identify specific authors and time periods; (2) to present desirable outcomes of the program; (3) to discuss alternatives for the sports to be included, types of events to be conducted, leadership roles, qualifications of coaches, and other pertinent aspects of the program; (4) to present problems that might be encountered; (5) to illustrate the continuing nature of the arguments throughout the years.

e. ARTICLES: 36-55.

7. Debate

a. TOPIC: *Pros and cons of athletic programs for females.*

b. PARTICIPANTS: Two teams of three or four students each.

c. FUNCTIONS: To represent physical educators from various time periods.

d. OBJECTIVES OF PRESENTATION: (1) To identify specific authors and time periods, (2) to present arguments supporting athletic programs for females, (3) to present arguments opposing such programs, (4) to illustrate the consistency of arguments throughout the years, (5) to convince the class members of the validity of the arguments; class members may vote at the conclusion of the presentation.

e. ARTICLES: 4, 56-61, 63, 64, 69, 70, 72, 77, 81, 82.

8. Drama

a. TOPIC: *Secondary school competitive athletics for females.*

b. PARTICIPANTS: Physical educators representing various time periods.

c. FUNCTIONS: To enact a meeting in which a secondary school athletic program for girls is planned and organized.

d. OBJECTIVES OF PRESENTATION: (1) To identify specific authors and time periods, (2) to present values of athletic experiences for girls, (3) to present problems that might be encountered, (4) to indicate the roles that women physical educators have played traditionally in this controversy, (5) to formulate policies by which the program should be governed, (6) to illustrate the consistency of the arguments throughout the years.

e. ARTICLES: 56-82.

9. Panel discussion

a. TOPIC: *History of athletics for females.*

b. PARTICIPANTS: Physical educators representing various time periods.

c. FUNCTIONS: To present information about women's's sports programs during each time period represented.

d. OBJECTIVES OF PRESENTATION: (1) To identify specific authors and time periods; (2) to discuss various aspects of women's sports programs, including societal attitudes, sports in which participation was allowed,

policies and regulations governing competition, types of events conducted, and problems encountered; (3) to entertain questions from class members.

e. ARTICLES: 66, 75, 80.

10. Panel discussion

a. TOPIC: *Implications of Title IX of the Education Amendments Act of 1972.*

b. PARTICIPANTS: Contemporary physical educators and coaches.

c. FUNCTIONS: To present information relative to the implications of Title IX for athletic programs for girls and women.

d. OBJECTIVES OF PRESENTATION: (1) To identify Title IX, (2) to explain the stipulations of Title IX with respect to intramural and athletic programs in the secondary schools, (3) to discuss the *separate but equal* concept, (4) to entertain questions from class members.

e. ARTICLES: 71 (refer to chapter 3), 74, 78, 79.

"Exercises may be devised for every age and for every degree of bodily strength, however reduced."
Johann Pestalozzi, 1820

CHAPTER FIVE

Physical education and the special child

One of the most visible and significant trends in modern society is the increased attention currently being accorded physically and mentally impaired individuals. Within the past decade, attitudes toward the capabilities of exceptional individuals have grown increasingly positive, and efforts to assist them in reaching realistic goals have opened doors to numerous avenues of achievement—doors that have been closed to them for centuries. These changes in attitude have implications for not only our personal lives but our professional perspectives as well.

The professional preparation of prospective physical educators would be incomplete without an introduction to several areas of concern directly related to the lives of individuals manifesting atypical characteristics. Toward this end, this chapter includes discussions of the following topics: (1) historical treatment of the exceptional individual; (2) legislation designed to enhance educational opportunities for individuals with handicapping conditions; (3) terminology associated with this legislation; and (4) implications of this legislation for physical education.

HISTORY*

We are witnessing the dawning of a new era for individuals with physical and mental impairments. The day has finally arrived when they may take their rightful places as contributing members of society. The picture has not always been so bright, however. Current attitudes toward the potentialities of these special populations and toward society's moral and educational obligations to them have evolved gradually over a span of many centuries. Only through an understanding of the inequities with which these individuals have contended historically can we begin to appreciate the significance of modern efforts to assist them in expanding their horizons.

In some primitive cultures, deformed children were considered to be liabilities

---

*Daniels, Arthur S., and Davies, Evelyn A.: Adapted physical education, New York, 1975, Harper & Row, Publishers, Inc., pp. 23-29.

to the welfare of the tribe. Since they were viewed as social burdens who could not contribute to the security of the tribe, they usually either died of neglect or were systematically destroyed.

As civilization developed, attitudes toward these individuals remained fairly stable. Individuals with handicapping conditions were considered to be unfit and were eliminated for several reasons. First, the people of these early cultures believed that they could improve the quality of society by destroying those who were considered abnormal. Second, the elimination of these individuals resulted in a reduction of the social and economic burdens that they represented. In addition, the fact that they were regarded as "works of Satan" contributed to the notion that they could be destroyed with impunity.

Before the coming of Christianity, there were many methods for eliminating atypical individuals. In India, they were thrown into rivers to drown. The Spartans of ancient Greece took deformed children to Mt. Taygetus and left them there on the slopes to die. The Athenians, reputed to be more kindly than the Spartans in their dispositions, merely allowed these children to die of neglect. In ancient Rome, the law permitted the fathers of deformed children to kill them shortly following birth. Eventually, Christian doctrine led to the dissipation of these practices to some extent, but negative attitudes lingered.

The Middle Ages brought some relief for individuals with handicapping conditions in that they were allowed to exist. Their function, however, was to amuse and entertain, and they frequently became court jesters or clowns. Although they served a social purpose, they still were regarded with superstition and fear because of the prevailing belief that they had been touched by Satan. Toward the end of the Renaissance, some progress toward humanitarianism was made, but the ancient concept of Satan's touch was perpetuated.

The Industrial Revolution of the eighteenth and nineteenth centuries was accompanied by a tremendous emphasis on economic gain. People were so busy manufacturing products and amassing wealth that they had little time for the unfortunates among them. Legal reform and medical advancements contributed to a degree of improvement, however, and in 1903 the first school for crippled children was opened in England.

In the United States, World War I is generally considered the turning point for special populations. The soldiers who returned injured and maimed from the battlefront awakened the American consciousness. As rehabilitation programs developed for these impaired veterans, attention gradually spread to serving the needs of civilians in similar straits.

In 1931, a White House Conference, conducted at the direction of President Herbert Hoover, recognized the rights of the child as the first rights of citizenship and published a list of 19 aims for the children of America. Among the aims to which the White House Conference pledged itself was the following:

For every child who is blind, deaf, crippled or otherwise physically handicapped, and for the child who is mentally handicapped, such measures as will early discover and diagnose his handicap, provide care and treatment, and so train him that he may become an asset to society rather than a liability. Expenses of these services should be borne publicly where they cannot be privately met.*

This expression of concern for handicapped children as well as the assertion that the public should be responsible for their welfare was a milestone in the progress of impaired individuals in the United States.

EDUCATION FOR ALL HANDICAPPED CHILDREN ACT OF 1975

The spirit of Hoover's White House Conference is reflected today in federal legislation designed to protect the rights of the impaired and to guarantee their access to equitable educational opportunities. On November 29, 1975, the Congress of the United States passed the Education for All Handicapped Children Act, also known as Public Law 94-142. The purpose of this act is:

to assure that all handicapped children have available to them . . . a free appropriate public education which emphasizes special education and related services designed to meet their unique needs, to assure that the rights of handicapped children and their parents or guardians are protected, to assist States and localities to provide for the education of all handicapped children, and to assess and assure the effectiveness of efforts to educate handicapped children.†

The important elements of PL 94-142 include the following: (1) a free appropriate public school education, (2) nondiscriminatory testing and assessment, (3) placement in the least restrictive environment, (4) preparation of individualized education programs (IEPs), (5) provisions for due process procedures, and (6) provision of related support services. The following definitions are presented to help you develop a better understanding of the provisions of this legislation.

Definitions

1. *Due process*—the right of the parents or guardians (a) to receive notice in writing before the school system takes (or recommends) any action that may change their child's school program or if the school refuses to take action to change the child's program; (b) to give or withhold permission for their child to be tested, evaluated, or placed in a specific program; (c) to see and examine and approve for accuracy all school records related to the identification, evaluation, and placement of their child; (d) to request an impartial due process hearing to protest any decision related to identification, evaluation, or placement of their

---

*White House Conference on Child Health and Protection: The children's charter, The Journal of Health and Physical Education **2**:23, March 1931.

†Education for All Handicapped Children Act of 1975, Public Law 94-142, U.S. Congress, Sec. 3c.

An understanding of the law is essential.

child; and (e) to appeal the results of the due process hearing to the State Department of Education and to the courts if they lose their case at the State level.*

2. *Free appropriate public education*—special education and related services that: (a) have been provided at public expense, under public supervision and direction, and without charge; (b) meet the standards of the State educational agency; (c) include an appropriate preschool, elementary, or secondary school education in the State involved; and (d) are provided in conformity with the individualized educational program.†

3. *Handicapped children*—those children who are evaluated as being mentally retarded, hard of hearing, deaf, speech impaired, visually handicapped, seriously

---

*Know your rights—and use them! Information from Closer Look, A Project of the Parents' Campaign for Handicapped Children and Youth, Washington, D.C., January 1979, p. 3.
†Op. cit., Education for All Handicapped Children Act of 1975, Sec. 4a (18).

emotionally disturbed, orthopedically impaired, other health impaired, deaf-blind, multihandicapped, or as having specific learning disabilities, who because of those impairments need special education and related services.*

4. *Individualized education program (IEP)* — a written statement for each handicapped child that includes: (a) a statement of the present levels of educational performance of such child; (b) a statement of annual goals, including short-term instructional objectives; (c) a statement of the specific educational services to be provided to such child and of the extent to which such child will be able to participate in regular educational programs; (d) the projected date for initiation and anticipated duration of such services; and (e) appropriate objective criteria and evaluation procedures and schedules for determining, on at least an annual basis, whether instructional objectives are being achieved.†

5. *Least restrictive environment* — each public agency shall ensure that: (a) to the maximum extent appropriate, handicapped children, including children in public or private institutions or other care facilities, are educated with children who are not handicapped; and (b) special classes, separate schooling, or other removal of handicapped children from the regular educational environment occurs only when the nature of the handicap is such that education in regular classes with the use of supplementary aids and services cannot be achieved satisfactorily.‡

6. *Non-discriminatory testing and assessment* — testing and evaluation materials and procedures used for the purposes of evaluation and placement of handicapped children must be selected and administered so they are not racially or culturally discriminatory.§

7. *Physical education* — the development of (a) physical and motor fitness; (b) fundamental motor skills and patterns; and (c) skills in aquatics, dance, and individual and group games and sports (including intramural and lifetime sports); it includes physical education, adapted physical education, movement education, and motor development.‖

8. *Related services* — transportation and such developmental, corrective, and other supportive services (including speech pathology and audiology, psychological services, physical and occupational therapy, recreation, and medical and counseling services, except that such medical services shall be for diagnostic and evaluation purposes only) as may be required to assist a handicapped child to benefit from special education, including the early identification and assessment of handicapping conditions in children.¶

---

*Department of Health, Education, and Welfare, Office of Education: Implementation of Part B of the Education of the Handicapped Act, Federal Register **42:**163, August 23, 1977, Sec. 121a.5 (a).
†Op. cit., Education for All Handicapped Children Act of 1975, Sec. 4a (19).
‡Op. cit., Department of Health, Education, and Welfare, Office of Education, Sec. 121a.550 (b).
§Ibid., Sec. 121a.530 (b).
‖Ibid., Sec. 121a.14 (a,2).
¶Op. cit., Education for All Handicapped Children Act of 1975, Sec. 4a (17).

Bowling may easily be adapted for visually impaired individuals.

9. *Special education*—specially designed instruction, at no cost to parents or guardians, to meet the unique needs of a handicapped child, including classroom instruction, instruction in physical education, home instruction, and instruction in hospitals and institutions.*

Physical education and PL 94-142

The primary provision of PL 94-142 is that, whenever appropriate, handicapped children must be integrated into the regular educational setting. This process is frequently referred to as *mainstreaming* and is among the most significant trends in education today. As a prospective physical educator, it is important for you to understand the implications of mainstreaming and to begin investigating the ways in which PL 94-142 will affect you and the students in your classes.

The initial area in which PL 94-142 has implications for you is in your professional preparation program. As you progress toward your goal of becoming a physical educator, you will study handicapping conditions in some detail. You will become aware of various ways in which to adapt physical education activities to the capabilities of physically or mentally impaired students. How might you help a blind child learn to run, swim, or play golf? Could basketball or baseball be adapted so that the orthopedically impaired child could derive as much pleasure from participation as the nonimpaired student? Could deaf students learn to dance and amputees learn to ski? What methods could be used to teach a cerebral palsied child to enjoy swimming and a mentally retarded child to ice-skate? Probably, you have experienced the presence of impaired students in your elementary and high school classes, and you could cite several ways in which you could adapt these activities to their capabilities. Specific professional preparation in this area will complement your previous experiences and should equip you with the skills and knowledge necessary to assist atypical students in reaching their physical potentials.

In addition to acquiring knowledge about the physical and mental conditions and capabilities of these students, you will also be exposed to information that should help you develop a deeper understanding of their individual needs and potentialities. You will investigate the physiological, psychological, and sociological implications of impairments and the contributions that physical education can make to the quality of life for impaired individuals. If physical education activities are beneficial for the nonhandicapped student, is there any reason to believe that the same activities would not be just as beneficial for the atypical student? Should these students be segregated from the rest of the students, or should they experience the more realistic atmosphere of the regular classroom? What are the physiological, psychological, and sociological implications of mainstreaming? Physical educators are obligated to discover answers to these questions. Only through

---

*Ibid., Sec. 4a (16).

WOOD COUNTY SCHOOLS
INDIVIDUAL EDUCATION PLAN

Name _____ School year _____ Age _____ Birth date _____

Parent's name _____ Address _____ Phone _____

District of residence _____ County _____ District of attendance _____ County _____

Conference date _____

I. Assessments completed	II. Statement of present levels of performances

III. Statement of the specific educational services

A. Special education services/programs

Eligible for	Recommendations	Starting date	Estimated time in program	Comments

B. Regular education services/programs   Comments:

IV. Annual goals	VI. Date and criteria for next review

The individual educational plan developed especially for your child will be reviewed at the end of the academic year, or earlier at your request, to evaluate its effectiveness in meeting your child's needs. At least 15 days prior to this review, as the child's parents, you will receive a notice that the review is scheduled and an invitation to participate in the conference.

VII. Committee members and titles

_____
(Chairperson)

_____

_____

_____

V. Indicate who, by titles or positions, will provide the short-term instructional objectives (which will be attached to this form upon completion).

VIII.

_____ I agree with this educational program and these services.

_____ I do not agree with this program.

_____
(Parent's signature)

_____
(Date)

knowledgeable, resourceful physical educators who are committed to serving the needs of *all* students can we provide a major contribution to the development of well-rounded, well-adjusted students, regardless of exceptional physical or mental characteristics.

In your professional preparation, you will also study PL 94-142 in greater detail and will learn of your responsibilities for complying with the law. The law is quite explicit in its expectations, and you will require a thorough understanding of its stipulations in order to fulfill your obligations. What is an IEP (see page 106), and what types of information must it contain? What is your role in the due process procedure? How can you assure nondiscriminatory testing and assessment? Compliance with PL 94-142 will require diligent study and serious thought if you are to implement its provisions accurately and intelligently.

The provisions of PL 94-142 require the inclusion of physical education in the handicapped child's curriculum. This stipulation virtually assures the continued existence of physical education programs in elementary and secondary schools and thus, indirectly, benefits all students. It assures all elementary and secondary school students the opportunity to experience those physical education activities that are essential to many aspects of their development. In addition, the presence of both handicapped and nonhandicapped children in the same setting should contribute to the development of a generation of youngsters who can see beyond physical and mental limitations to the inherent talents and capabilities of all individuals.

SUMMARY

Although history demonstrates that handicapped citizens have been subjected to harsh and inequitable treatment in many civilizations, modern society recognizes and accepts moral and educational obligations to impaired individuals. Passage of the Education for All Handicapped Children Act of 1975 (Public Law 94-142) represents a significant landmark in the progress toward assuring equal rights for all those citizens manifesting handicapping conditions. The basic provision of this legislation is that all handicapped children must be educated, to the fullest extent feasible, with nonhandicapped children. As a physical educator, you will be expected to fulfill your obligations to these children as well as to nonimpaired children.

Although legislation mandating equal educational opportunities for handicapped children is relatively recent, physical educators have been addressing themselves to this topic for many years. Historically, our profession has been committed to providing handicapped children with quality education and to preparing prospective physical educators to work with these special populations. Why have physical educators recognized the importance of physical activity for the handicapped? What are the benefits of physical education for exceptional children? Are there physiological, psychological, and sociological implications to be considered? What are the advantages and disadvantages of mainstreaming

Swimming is a popular activity.

these children into the regular educational environment? How will you decide which children should be mainstreamed and which children will require special classes? How will you adapt your regular programs to meet their needs? What problems will you face in attempting to meet the needs of *all* the children in your classes? How can you best prepare yourself to make the most significant contributions to the lives of all students? Through your research of the literature, you will find answers to many of these questions. You will also discover that physical educators of the past initiated many of the ideas that are currently receiving widespread acceptance. As you study this important aspect of your professional preparation, the advice of Julian Stein, a recognized authority on programs for the handicapped, may be beneficial:

First steps in implementing the spirit of mainstreaming are taking stock of one's own personal attitudes about special people, realizing that to individualize one must know the individual, and recognizing that a difference is a difference only when it makes a difference.*

---

*Stein, Julian: Sense and nonsense about mainstreaming, The Journal of Physical Education and Recreation **47**:43, January 1976.

1 WHAT THE PROFESSIONAL NEEDS TO CONSIDER BEFORE EMBARKING ON PROGRAMS OF RESEARCH AND DEMONSTRATION NEEDS FOR THE PHYSICALLY HANDICAPPED*

By Timothy J. Nugent
*Professor and Director, Division of Rehabilitation-Education Services,
Rehabilitation Education Center, University of Illinois, Champaign*

If there is justification for physical education and recreation in the life of anyone then it is even more justified in the life of the individual who has lost a portion of his physical well-being and who, because of apathy, attitudinal barriers, and physical barriers has been prone to inactivity or has had inactivity unjustly imposed upon him. The physical implications and advantages of physical activity are readily recognized; the social and psychological benefits are not so readily identified nor as easily evaluated, but they occur also.

Through participation in physical activities and recreation, the individual with a disability does (1) realize self-identification (even self-justification), (2) overcome self-consciousness, (3) develop self-confidence, (4) have the opportunity to express emotion naturally, (5) have the opportunity to respond to successes and failures, (6) develop a concept of self which is fundamental to each of us if we are to move forward with any measure of success, and (7) have the opportunity for self-evaluation along with self-satisfaction.

Before professionals embark on programs of research and demonstration needs in physical education and recreation for the physically handicapped, there is great need to make the following points.

1. There should be greater involvement of individuals with disabilities in ongoing programs. There is a basic reason for this. Their lack of involvement and the nothingness which has surrounded them is the basis for their present con-

cept of self. Therefore, when questioned or observed they tend to reflect this nothingness or to reflect the attitudes of those about them. They have met so many denials or have been made to feel that they cannot do so many things, that studies and observations without involvement would tend to come up with incomplete, if not totally wrong, answers.

2. There should be more involvement on the part of professional people who will engage in research and demonstration so that they can distinguish between that which is real and that which is the manifestation of limitations and impositions upon the individual with a disability.

3. We must have more interdisciplinary studies. We must not approach this problem from the perspective of a singular discipline and thereby further segment the individual. There is much greater need for interdisciplinary relationships and studies relating to all aspects of individual growth and development as each contributes to the other. Only when we make this approach will we really find the answers to what, when, where, why, and how.

4. We must have greater emphasis on demonstration where there has been leadership to make known what these individuals can do and how they can do it. We will not then be spending so much time, money, and effort on studies which will merely put us at the threshold.

5. We must not consider individuals with disabilities categorically and by name of the disability, per se, but by functional concepts. We know, quite conclusively, that individuals with many causes of disability (various diseases and various types of injury) are functionally compati-

*From Journal of Health, Physical Education, and Recreation **40:**47-48, May 1969.

ble and are effectively helpful to each other and in total program success. To assume that a person with a given title or identification of disability must function in a given way is as wrong as assuming that all fat people are lazy and all redheads are temperamental.

6. In designing or constructing our programs and in designing or constructing the facilities to accommodate these programs we should design for the functioning of the individual and not in such a way as to force the individual to function within the limits of the design.

7. We must recognize that certain settings, particularly well defined institutional settings and domiciliary care centers, are themselves limiting to the individual and therefore place limitations on the results of certain research, demonstration, and study. It is of paramount importance that we get individuals with disabilities involved in programs in normal environs with normal objectives and normal reciprocities of people with people and people with things if the studies are to be meaningful.

8. Last but not least, we should look vigorously about us to see what is already being done. As an example, neurologically and orthopedically handicapped persons, including the very involved high level manifestations such as quadriplegia and quadriparesis are already participating in wheelchair football, wheelchair basketball, wheelchair baseball, wheelchair track and field, wheelchair archery, wheelchair fencing, wheelchair square dancing, wheelchair bowling, some forms of gymnastics, swimming, golf, and many lesser activities. The blind are participating in bowling, wrestling, swimming, dancing, baseball, and many lesser activities. More important, they are participating in these things in normal settings with very few deviations from normal rules of competition. For the most part it is necessary only to change those rules that relate to how one gets about.

a. The National Wheelchair Basketball Association is 21 years old and has held 21 successful annual tournaments. The Association is made up of seven conferences and 44 teams from coast to coast. The records are comparable and in some instances better than, intercollegiate records. They play by NCAA rules with only two modifications and one addition.

b. For twelve years there has been national competition in track and field, archery, swimming, bowling, table tennis, and other sports, known as the National Wheelchair Games. The severely disabled and the lesser disabled, young and old, throughout the United States are very much involved and look forward each year to the National Wheelchair Games.

c. Since 1952 there has been international competition in almost all of these activities. Beginning with two countries, competition has grown to include more than 400 athletes with physical disabilities, from over 30 nations, who have qualified through vigorous local and national competitions.

Yet, few of our professional people are aware of these things, few have seen any of these activities, and even fewer are themselves engaged in these activities. It is an indictment of the professions of recreation and physical education that almost all of these groups have been founded by, are managed by, and are coached by laymen. The municipal and/or school physical education and recreation programs and personnel are seldom, if ever, involved. Where are our professionals? Whenever difficulties are encountered by any of these groups, it is more often than not attributable to lack of good professional leadership. On the other hand, some of these laymen are doing a better job than professionals might be expected to do.

At the Rehabilitation Education Center we have already been privileged to do or are doing many basic studies in areas such as attitudes, motivation, social significance (values), psychological factors, energy expenditure, heart function and response, qualitative and quantitative evaluations of cardiovascular function and response with particular emphasis on peripheral circulation, respiratory function and response, follow-up studies, and specific skills and activities. It is amazing what we have already learned, and yet we have only begun to scratch the surface.

Although recreation to the individual participant might be, and should be, recreation for the sake of recreation itself, we, as professional people, would be naive and short-sighted not to recognize that we have a tool with which many things can be learned and which might accomplish many things in the interest of individuals with physical disabilities. All other services within our program benefit from our student's involvement in physical and recreational activities. We can readily note the success of those who do participate as against the troubles of those who do not, although at times it might be a delayed action.

Because of the position in which so many individuals with disabilities have found themselves, because of attitudinal barriers and man-made physical barriers which have excluded them from those things that we all take for granted, they so often don't or can't reflect what would otherwise be their normal aspirations, interests, and abilities. Therefore, involvement is a fundamental necessity.

Let us in our research, demonstration, and program development find the means to include individuals with disabilities in normal environs, in a normal manner, in normal and acceptable activities from which we might logically expect normal responses and benefits and thereby add dimension and meaning to our efforts. We must become ever more sensitive to this concept.

---

2 WHAT'S IN A LABEL?*

By Molly C. Gorelick
Associate Professor and Preschool Project Director in the Pre-School Laboratory, California State University—Northridge, Northridge, California

Twenty-five years ago I accepted my first teaching position. By choice, I requested a class of mentally retarded children. Some of my professors tried to discourage me from this choice, saying that I would be wasting my talents. But I disagreed with them. I was a psychology major and I felt that I could learn more about learning from teaching children who were reputed to have difficulty in learning. I felt that the bright children would learn in spite of me—but the retarded would really put my skill as a teacher to the test.

The first thing I learned from the educable mentally retarded was that the term Mentally Retarded was a label that told me very little about each individual child except perhaps that his I.Q. fell between 50 and 75, plus or minus a probable error of five points. The label EMR did not tell me that Manuel could solve problems in construction that were beyond my comprehension or that Margaret could draw beautiful designs, or that Ralph's social competencies and sensitivity to others were to be envied.

As special education programs proliferated in the years that followed, we started to label more children and we segregated them from the mainstream of childhood, all in our sincere effort to help them. In California we had created approximately 29 different special categories and proceeded to focus in on the child's disability—his handicap. This emphasis on the child's handicap led to stereotyped conceptions of children who possessed these handicaps. We called them retarded, blind, deaf, cerebral palsied, as if their total physiology, their cognitive and emotional functioning could be described by those labels. We failed to advertise their many abilities and talents.

After teaching retarded children I taught classes of children labeled "bright," "gifted," "slow learners," etc. I found that there was no such thing as a homogeneous class of children, no matter what their label or age. Each child, regardless of his label, has a unique profile of abilities and disabilities. It is time we emphasized abilities rather than disabilities.

Another truth I learned was that our basic knowledge about how human beings learn applies to all children, that there are no magic teaching formulas and methods which will work for all children or only for special children, that the good teacher assesses each child's strengths and weaknesses and then selects the methods appropriate for that child. Thus, it is encumbent upon those of us who are training teachers to ground prospective teachers well in a wide repertoire of teaching styles and methods. Those who are in teaching should continually add new approaches to their existing repertoire so as to be able to reach the individual child.

In September 1971 at California State University, Northridge I initiated a project to train teachers at the preschool level to work in nursery schools integrating children with handicaps.

Our first problem, when we integrated children with a handicap such as Downs syndrome, deaf-

*From Journal of Health, Physical Education, and Recreation **45**:71-72, September 1974.

ness, blindness, or cerebral palsy into the existing University nursery school, was teacher uncertainty. They asked, "What do I do with the deaf child?" My answer was, "What do you do with any child who is new to a class?" "How do you communicate if you are in a foreign country? Try that with the deaf child." The teachers were insecure, fearful about their ability to deal with a little child who came to them with a label. Teachers who were considered superior and experienced were suddenly unsure of their teaching abilities; they felt they lacked the skill and training to handle a child with a handicap. Thus, before we can succeed in integrating children, we will have to overcome this insecurity and attitude that only specialized experts can work with children with handicaps.

Those of you who now have children in your classes who are blind, deaf, retarded, or with other handicaps have found that these children ride the same tricycles, climb the same jungle gyms, lick their fingers after stirring some delicious mixture, throw sand, hug you or taunt you—in other words, they really are children.

We have to develop a new/old breed of teachers who, like the teacher in the little red school house, can assess each child and plan individualized programs for the wide spectrum of abilities found in a single classroom.

The preschool is a wonderful place to begin the integration of children. Young children can and do accept differences in race, creed, or handicap if their teachers, parents, and the community serve as models for such acceptance and eliminate their own fears of differences. We can greatly reduce segregation of children if we break down the mental barriers we have built up concerning differences. Of course, there will be some children for whom special classes are needed. Too frequently when we change our direction in education we throw the baby out with the bath water. Let's not eliminate all special nursery classes or specialists, but let's look at children as individuals and make placements accordingly.

Above all, let's examine our own fears and prejudices honestly. For example, teachers say, "Won't the blind child or the deaf child take an inordinate amount of teacher time? Won't the other children be neglected?" This can happen but shouldn't. Each child in that classroom needs attention; to provide it, you use assistant teachers, parent aides, high school aides, and community volunteers. Let's not forget that the chil-

dren themselves can be taught to help each other, even at this young age. For example, the children in our program quickly imitated the teacher and would turn the hard of hearing child's face toward them when they wanted to speak to him. They would guide the blind child by saying, "Listen to my voice, Kyle" or "Here, touch this, Kyle."

One mother reported that her four-year-old son, hearing that their old sick dog couldn't bark anymore, suggested that he could teach the dog some sign language. A volunteer who had been tutoring the deaf child had taught the other children in the class some signing.

I believe we now have a tentative (nothing is as constant as change) training model which is successful in making our young trainees and experienced head teachers feel comfortable and competent to teach in the integrated program.

Following is an excerpt from a letter we received from a former head teacher in our program who left to direct a county Head Start program in central California just a short time ago. When we first integrated children into our program, this creative, fine, and experienced teacher was convinced that she and the program were going to be detrimental to the blind child and the deaf child we had enrolled. She was in the integrated program about three years before she left to assume her new position. The following is a quote from her first letter to her former colleagues: "This coming week we are having an inservice workshop, and the topic is—guess what? Integrating the handicapped child into the normal preschool classroom. They didn't have anyone to lead the workshop, so guess who is going to do it? Right! Me!"

Another head teacher wrote: "When I first learned of the implementation and goals of the integrated program, my initial reaction was 'It's impossible! Teachers must have special training to work with handicapped children. I won't know how to meet their needs.'

"After two years as a supervising teacher in the program, I have learned that it *is* possible. Not only have I learned it, the concept of the integrated program has become an important element in my educational philosophy. Because when it comes to actual classroom implementation, the goal becomes individualization, the creation of a learning environment where the abilities of each child are assessed, individualized objectives and learning opportunities are designed, so that each child may grow and develop as much as he can in the length of time he is a class member."

In summary, in our preschool project we call our teachers developmental teachers because we want to train young people to appreciate and understand the similarities and differences in the development of all children. We want these teachers to feel competent in providing a variety of learning opportunities which will permit the children to develop and grow according to their own individual profile of abilities. We hope that these teachers and you too will help eliminate the segregation and minority status of many children with handicaps and return them to the mainstream of childhood.

3 A LOOK AT STIGMAS AND THE ROLES OF RECREATORS AND PHYSICAL EDUCATORS*

By Mariann Soulek

"Handicapped" is the limitation that I—or other people—feel that the disability imposes on me which affects doing what I *need* to do, doing what I *want* to do, and *being* what I want to be. Should we, the physically impaired, develop healthy emotional relationships and be able to use what remains in place of those parts which are absent or not functioning, our chances are good for accomplishing a normal life. We have overcome the psychological loss and can cope with the attitudes of society.

Two major factors determine the behavioral pattern of a person with a physical impairment: psychological and sociological considerations. The psychological factors deal with the perception of self-concept, self-esteem, and self-respect. Psychological factors define the role we, the physically impaired, play in society. The sociological factors are those outside oneself: the way society responds toward a group or individual. Social barriers result from a variety of factors, including stigma, prejudice, and discrimination. These factors are instrumental in the development and maintenance of the role in which we, the physically impaired, find ourselves in an able-bodied world.

Both the psychological and sociological factors are so interrelated in their influence upon us that it is difficult to determine which is the more dominant. Studies have indicated that when both factors are favorable physical impairment may not cause maladjustment and we do not become "handicapped."

Those in recreation and physical education should consider the nature of prejudice that has stigmatized the physically disabled as "handicapped" and has reduced us to second class citizenship. To a degree we are what people think of us. If we are constantly reminded both in words and in actions that we are dependent we will *be* dependent. Society has placed the physically impaired in a minority role by its attitudes toward physical impairment; a well-developed stigma has resulted in prejudice and discrimination. We have reacted and, in many cases performed according to what society has expected.

The goals of recreators and physical educators should be set toward integrating the physically impaired into community life. By understanding the nature of the prejudice and some of the social factors in its formation, better programming and placement can be made. A better life for the physically impaired can result.

Society has not kept abreast of the results of modern medicine and rehabilitation and the capabilities for restoration of the psychological and physical deficiencies produced by physical impairments. It is important for recreators and physical educators to know of the diminished differences between the physically impaired and the able-bodied and to incorporate these advances within their programs.

Attitudes growing out of the mores of our soci-

*From The Journal of Physical Education and Recreation **46**:28-29, May 1975.

ety stigmatize us and become stereotyped beliefs. The stigma implies that physical disability is a trait that discredits us by spoiling both our identity and our respectability. It allows moral implications about our character and our personality. Society's attitudes toward the physically impaired mesh into a pattern that results in prejudice, then discrimination. Recreators and physical educators are involved with propagating these attitudes when segregation, not integration, is the intent of their programs. Even labels are important, for they form linguistic factors that reinforce the attitudes encountered by the physically impaired. Terms such as "crippled" and "handicapped" help make the physically impaired different from the normal society, for we are what people believe us to be.

Discrimination is the acting out of prejudice. Discrimination in education, recreation, and other social and economic benefits is the overt form of a prejudiced attitude of rejection from the ingroup represented by the able-bodied world. The physically impaired person grows up surrounded by prejudiced physical and attitudinal standards set by the able-bodied.

The whole stigma, prejudice, and discrimination cycle has affected physical education curriculums. The teaching of skills, recreation programs, and the provision of space and programs to use learned skills has been adversely affected.

I would like to believe that physical educators and recreators are interested and care enough to break down the barriers that separate the physically impaired from the able-bodied world. I see the physical educators and recreators playing a vital role in helping us become a member of the in-group.

How can you help? Through the programs you offer!

The physical educator paves the way by teaching the skills. We need to introduce the physically impaired to more team sports and physical activities, such as water polo, square dancing, soccer, volleyball, basketball, softball, and football, to name a few. Swimming, bowling, archery, table tennis, field events, and weight lifting are but a few of the individual and dual sports that should receive greater attention in physical education classes. The recreator is responsible for providing the programs for the continued use of learned skills in a social setting within the community. The recreator should be concerned with integrative activities for fun, for competition. The recreator must put emphasis on sustaining activities that will allow carry over and will integrate us into community programs with the able-bodied as well as our peers.

In order for the physically impaired to achieve the status of being one of the in-group, we need to learn and then do the same kinds of things the in-group learns and does. Sounds simple enough, but why is this not happening? No longer should the physically impaired be relegated to secondary positions because the physical educator says "I don't know how," or the recreator says "I don't know what to program." Adapted, remedial, and corrective physical education programs need to be expanded into more elementary and secondary school programs. There needs to be more emphasis on integrative skills. Community recreation programs must broaden their offerings and work toward the integration of the physically impaired into existing programs. In addition, assisting services are needed in order to increase the participation of the physically impaired in regular programs. The key to success is in having trained individuals to conduct the programs. Individuals are needed who can cope with prejudice and understand discrimination and who, in their wise leadership, can attend to destroying the myths that separate the physically impaired from the able-bodied.

One challenge is to teach skills—a broad range of leisure skills including individual, dual, and team sports, diverse outdoor physical skills, as well as the all too common "passive" activities. The second challenge is to provide community resources and opportunities for continuing enjoyment of leisure participation. Breaking down the barriers and expanding the in-group is the responsibility of everyone.

SUPPLEMENTAL READINGS
1930-1939

4. Lommen, Olga: School programs for the handicapped, The Journal of Health and Physical Education **9:**350-352, 390, June 1938.
5. White House Conference on Child Health and Protection: The children's charter, The Journal of Health and Physical Education **2:**23, March 1931.

1940-1949

6. Richardson, Jean: Physical education for all students, The Journal of Health and Physical Education **13:**587, 616-618, December 1942.

1950-1959

7. American Association for Health, Physical Education, and Recreation: Guiding principles for adapted physical education, The Journal of the American Association for Health, Physical Education, and Recreation **23:**15, 28, April 1952.
8. Sellwood, J. J.: The relationship of physical education and recreation to basic needs of the handicapped, The Physical Educator **12:**19, March 1955.
9. Stafford, George T.: Should your handicapped child participate in physical education? The Physical Educator **12:**60-62, May 1955.

1960-1969

10. Adapted physical education, Journal of Health, Physical Education, and Recreation **40:**45-46, May 1969.
11. Gart, Wally: An adapted physical education program in a new senior high school, Journal of Health, Physical Education, and Recreation **40:**49-51, May 1969.
12. Schoon, John R.: Some psychological factors in motivating handicapped students in adapted physical education, The Physical Educator **19:**138-140, December 1962.
13. Welch, Paula, and Pangle, Roy: Physi-

cal education and the EMR; separate vs regular classes, The Physical Educator **24:**102-104, October 1967.

1970-1979

14. Clarification of terms, Journal of Health, Physical Education, and Recreation **42:**63-66, 68, September 1971.
15. Jansma, Paul: Get ready for mainstreaming! The Journal of Physical Education and Recreation **48:**15-16, September 1977.
16. Lloyd, Marcia L.: The handicapped can dance, too, The Journal of Physical Education and Recreation **49:**52-53, May 1978.
17. Moseley, M. Louise, and Wills, Suzzane E.: Eliminate the exclusion principle, Journal of Health, Physical Education, and Recreation **41:**28, September 1970.
18. Osternig, Louis R., and Santomier, James P.: Public Law 94-142; implications for professional preparation, The Physical Educator **35:**75-77, May 1978.
19. Priest, Louise: Integrating the disabled into aquatics programs, The Journal of Physical Education and Recreation **50:** 57, 59, February 1979.
20. Stein, Julian: Sense and nonsense about mainstreaming, The Journal of Physical Education and Recreation **47:**43, January 1976.
21. Winnick, Joseph P.: Techniques for integration, The Journal of Physical Education and Recreation **49:**22, June 1978.

ASSIGNMENTS
Individual activities

1. Prepare a list of benefits that participation in physical education activities could provide for mentally or physically impaired individuals.
   ARTICLES: 1, 3, 7-10, 12, 16.
2. Explain the concept of mainstreaming and indicate the benefits of integrating physically or mentally impaired individuals into regular physical education classes.

ARTICLES: 2-9, 13, 14, 16-18, 20, 21.

3. Suggest measures that could be undertaken to assist present and future physical educators in developing the expertise necessary to work with impaired individuals.

ARTICLES: 1, 15, 18, 19, 21.

Group presentations

1. Panel discussion
   a. TOPIC: *Mainstreaming.*
   b. PARTICIPANTS: Physical educators representing various time periods and different points of view.
   c. FUNCTIONS: To discuss the pros and cons of mainstreaming impaired individuals into regular physical education classes.
   d. OBJECTIVES OF PRESENTATION: (1) To identify specific authors and time periods, (2) to explain PL 94-142, (3) to present arguments supporting the concept of mainstreaming, (4) to present arguments supporting the segregation of impaired students, (5) to illustrate the consistency of arguments throughout the years.
   e. ARTICLES: 2-7, 9, 13, 14, 16, 19-21.
2. Drama
   a. TOPIC: *Initiation of an adapted physical education program in a school.*
   b. PARTICIPANTS: Adapted physical educators representing various time periods.
   c. FUNCTIONS: To enact a meeting in which an integrated physical education program is being planned and organized.
   d. OBJECTIVES OF PRESENTATION: (1) To identify specific authors and time periods; (2) to identify objectives of the integrated program; (3) to identify problems that might be encountered in organizing and conducting the program; (4) to suggest solutions to the problems; (5) to illustrate similarities among the attitudes, objectives, and problems of earlier years and those of modern times.
   e. ARTICLES: 1, 3, 4, 6-13, 15, 16, 19-21.
3. Panel discussion
   a. TOPIC: *Contributions of physical education activities.*
   b. PARTICIPANTS: Physical educators representing various time periods.
   c. FUNCTIONS: To discuss the contributions of physical education activities to the lives of impaired individuals.
   d. OBJECTIVES OF PRESENTATION: (1) To identify specific authors and time periods, (2) to identify specific contributions of physical education activities to the lives of impaired individuals, (3) to identify various physical education activities and present suggestions relative to their adaptation for impaired students, (4) to illustrate the consistency of viewpoints throughout the years.
   e. ARTICLES: 1, 3, 7-9, 12, 16.

CHAPTER SIX

Career opportunities

"I will study and get ready, and perhaps my chance will come."
Abraham Lincoln

When you decided to major in physical education, you may have envisioned becoming a physical educator or an athletic coach, or both, in the school setting. These are the careers that have been selected by most physical education graduates. During your early experiences in physical education preparation, you may find it beneficial to ask yourself several questions about your career choice and, possibly, to investigate alternative professions that will be available to you. For example: Why do you want to become a teacher? At which level of education do you wish to teach? Elementary school? Secondary school? The college level? What are the academic degree requirements for teaching at each of these levels? Do you wish to pursue graduate study? What are your alternatives if you decide that you do not wish to become a teacher? Does teaching occur only in the school setting? Must all physical education graduates become teachers? What other careers might your professional preparation experiences in physical education equip you to pursue?

The information presented in this chapter is designed to enhance your understanding of the roles of physical educators and coaches in the schools. In addition, you will be introduced to professional possibilities that traditionally have not been included among career alternatives for physical education graduates.

TEACHING

In view of the fact that you have been a student for at least 12 years and have been in contact with a variety of teachers and teaching situations, you probably have a fairly good idea of what is involved in "teaching school." In fact, this knowledge of the teaching profession and the rewards it promises may have been what led you to consider a teaching career. What is it about the teaching profession that appeals to you? What attributes do you possess that you believe would contribute to your effectiveness as a teacher? Indeed, what attributes should a good teacher possess?

Research demonstrates that there exists no simple definition of a good teacher—no list of characteristics that we can check off and evaluate—no way to declare with any certainty that one individual will be or another individual will not be a good teacher. The relationship between each teacher and each student takes unique form, in direct response to the individuality of both participants. This characteristic of the educational process permits teachers to pursue their goals and objectives in a personalized manner and to choose those teaching styles and techniques for which they are best suited. It is difficult, therefore, to predict success in the teaching profession, and the choice of teaching as a career must be based on other factors, many of which are personal.

Since there is no simple definition of a good teacher, the wisest course of action appears to be that you begin by examining your attitudes toward students at different levels of education and toward the responsibilities of the teaching profession. Such an examination might help you determine if teaching is the profession

Elementary school teaching requires special skills.

for you. Do you like and enjoy children at either the elementary school or the secondary school level? Do you prefer being associated with young adults at the college level? Do you derive pleasure from sharing your knowledge and expertise with others? How do you feel about financial rewards? Are they significant enough to influence your career choice? Are you aware of the many responsibilities that accompany the teaching profession, and are you willing to accept them?

There are many other questions that you could pose, and they may become apparent to you as you explore the teaching profession in greater depth. The most important factor, however, is that you begin to understand the teaching profession and to make some realistic decisions about your choice of teaching as a career.

Elementary school

There is little disagreement in the education profession that the teaching and learning occurring at the elementary school level represent some of the most crucial experiences in education. It is here that the foundation is laid for future development and accomplishment. For most children, elementary school represents the initial experience away from home for any significant time. From the day that children enter the first grade until they graduate from high school or college, they will spend more hours in the school environment than they will spend in the home. What a responsibility for elementary school teachers! Not only must they be knowledgeable and skilled in conveying factual information, but they must also understand principles of child growth and development, be prepared to act as parent substitutes in moments of distress, and be willing to devote many hours to the nurture of young minds and bodies. Only those individuals who are genuinely suited to work with this age group should consider accepting the challenge.

How do you feel about teaching at the elementary school level? Do you enjoy being with young children? Do they fascinate and inspire you? Would you welcome the opportunity to assist them in developing mental and physical prowess, or do you find their lack of expertise and sophistication annoying? Is patience one of your virtues? In attempting to answer these questions, you may find it beneficial to try recalling your days in elementary school. The memories may have faded with time, however, and you may find it necessary to visit the elementary school classroom to obtain a more realistic picture of these children and the setting in which they learn and grow. A very special personality is required for teaching elementary school children, and all aspects of this endeavor should be explored before you determine whether elementary school teaching is the area in which you wish to pursue your professional goals.

Secondary school

Your experiences in junior high and high school are probably relatively fresh in your memory. As you reflect on the attitudes and behaviors of you and your classmates during those years, how do you assess your ability to interact with

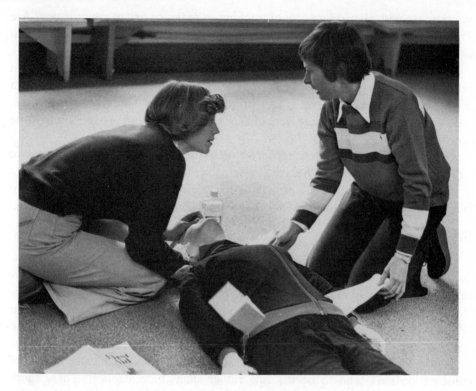

Physical educators may teach a variety of activities.

secondary school students? Secondary school teachers work with adolescents who are striving to become independent in both thought and action but who, at the same time, are clinging to the security of the comfortable and the familiar. Adolescence represents a crisis in the lives of many young people, and the secondary school teacher must be prepared to recognize and deal with this fact and its accompanying problems. Adolescents are exciting and challenging. Their skills are more highly developed than those of elementary school students, and their degree of sophistication has increased markedly. Discipline problems may be greater in secondary school, but if you are prepared both intellectually and psychologically to confront and solve these problems, the rewards of working with adolescents can be great.

Secondary school represents the termination of the educational process for many students. Secondary school teachers are responsible for equipping these students with skills and knowledges necessary to pursue lives and careers of their own. Does the prospect of this responsibility appeal to you? Are you attracted to working with emerging young adults? Do discipline problems frighten you or challenge you? How do you feel about preparing students to face life? Again, as was the case with elementary school teaching, is patience one of your virtues? Are you invigorated by overt expressions of growth or turned off by students who attempt to assert their individuality?

Perhaps a few visits to several junior high or high schools will help you reach a better understanding of "the view from the other side of the desk." Being a teacher at the secondary level is far different from being a student at that level, and observations of secondary school teachers and students in action could be beneficial to you.

Good secondary school teachers are vital to the future of the American way of life, and strong, capable teachers are in demand. If you have a genuine liking and respect for this age group and are willing to accept the challenges, you may find that secondary school is the level of education at which you will be most effective.

Higher education

The most obvious difference between elementary or secondary school students and students in college is that college students usually are in school by virtue of their own choices. In most cases, they have made thoughtful and conscious decisions to attend college. Each student may have different reasons for continuing the educational process, but they are not coerced—no state law requires their presence. At the college level, discipline problems are usually fewer, skill development may have reached a more advanced stage, and higher intelligence levels and conscientiousness tend to be the rule rather than the exception. These facts, combined with the students' greater maturity and sophistication, are enticements to teaching at the college level.

College teachers fulfill a variety of roles. Among the tasks that they may be called on to perform are teaching, coaching, curriculum development, public service, research, and publication. These areas involve somewhat different functions.

College physical education teaching extends over many subject areas and academic levels. At the undergraduate level, physical educators may teach the general physical education activity courses that are required of or offered to all university students. These teachers may instruct professional preparation courses offered to physical education major or minor students. College teachers may also work with graduate students who are pursuing master's or doctoral degrees. Coaching an athletic team is frequently included in the job assignment of college physical educators.

Curriculum development is a significant feature of college teaching. Faculty members are responsible for designing and implementing undergraduate and graduate physical education professional preparation programs as well as general physical education programs. Developing curricula requires not only an in-depth knowledge of curriculum planning but also the willingness to devote many hours to designing sound programs that meet the current needs of the students.

A rare moment of solitude.

Public service involves sharing professional knowledge and expertise with the general public on a local, state, regional, national, or international level. Examples of such service include conducting workshops for community groups, directing athletic events for various public agencies such as the Scouts, and speaking to interest groups about areas of professional concern.

Research in physical education offers a myriad of possibilities. Teachers might conduct meaningful research in many areas pertinent to physical education, such as teaching methodology, exercise physiology, motor learning, and any of the other specialized areas included in the profession. As you continue in your professional preparation program, you will become more aware of the nature of these areas of study and may develop an interest in researching them further.

College teachers also contribute to the profession through textbooks, instructors' manuals, articles, research reports, book reviews, abstracts, and a variety of other forms of publications. Publication is time consuming and requires vast stores of energy and perseverance. Most college teachers are, however, expected to contribute to the profession and to the public through some type of publication.

All physical educators, regardless of the level at which they teach, may be involved with each of the aforementioned areas. These endeavors are not specific to college teaching. Most institutions of higher learning, however, expect faculty members to participate in teaching, public service, research, and publication. Since involvement in these pursuits frequently is a prerequisite to professional advancement and financial rewards at the college level, a commitment to them is essential to the consideration of college teaching as a career.

The December 1966 issue of *Quest* is devoted to an investigation of the college physical educator as administrator, artist, author, coach, graduate adviser, evaluator, researcher, professor, and teacher. Perhaps an examination of the responsibilities of these roles will clarify the functions of the college physical educator and will assist you in determining your professional directions.

Athletic coaching

Teachers at all levels of education frequently are afforded opportunities to coach athletic teams. Coaching, a form of teaching, is fast becoming a popular field for young graduates. Qualified and dedicated coaches are essential to the development of sound athletic programs.

If you have participated on an interscholastic or intercollegiate athletic team, you probably are aware of many of the duties and responsibilities of coaches. There is much more to coaching than putting the team on the court or on the field on game day. Successful coaching requires many hours of work and preparation behind the scenes, and frequently these efforts are unnoticed by spectators and players alike.

Are you interested in the challenges that accompany coaching? Are you willing to devote much of your personal time to the development of young athletes? Do you subscribe to the win-at-all-cost philosophy and regard a winning season as a vehicle for the enhancement of your ego? Or do you believe that coaching involves the development of young people into better athletes and better human beings? Coaching and the goals of athletic programs are discussed in some detail in Chapter 4. An investigation of the literature associated with the topic and an exploration of the responsibilities of coaches may help you determine whether coaching should be included among your professional goals.

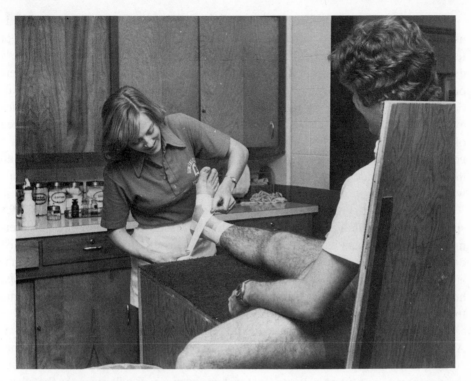

Athletic trainers have serious responsibilities.

Many states require coaching certification. If you decide to pursue coaching as a career, you would be wise to investigate these requirements and to prepare yourself to meet them by taking the requisite courses leading to a coaching major, minor, or certificate.

GRADUATE STUDY

You may be among the growing number of students planning to continue your education beyond the undergraduate degree. Regardless of whether that is your current plan, you should be aware of the opportunities available to you in graduate school. In addition, an understanding of the academic degree requirements for teaching at various levels of education might influence your decision relative to graduate study.

Teaching at the elementary or secondary school level usually requires a bachelor's degree, the undergraduate degree. Frequently, financial rewards are increased as teachers earn additional academic credits and degrees. This fact, coupled with the expectation that educators will further their own education in some way, prompts many elementary school and secondary school teachers to attend graduate school.

The initial graduate degree is the *master's degree*. Although this degree is usually a prerequisite to teaching at the college level, a growing number of teachers at all levels of education are becoming interested in earning the master's degree. The areas of study that you might pursue at the master's level are numerous. You need only to browse through the graduate catalogues of several institutions to become aware of the vast number of specialties and subspecialties available to a physical education graduate student. You may wish to study an area of particular interest to you, or you may wish to develop your capabilities as a generalist to a greater extent. Whatever you desire, you should be able to find an institution that meets your needs. Your personal interests and professional goals will be important in the determination of your choice.

The *specialist degree* is currently gaining in popularity. Many institutions offer specialist degrees that are awarded upon the successful completion of a predetermined number of academic credits beyond the master's degree. Most specialist degrees are involved with education, or some aspect of education such as administration, rather than with physical education specifically. In spite of the emphasis, however, you may find that this degree fits into your career plans and represents the appropriate course of study for you to pursue.

The *doctoral degree* is considered the terminal degree in physical education. Although some college teaching jobs require only the master's degree, it is becoming increasingly difficult to secure a stable college teaching position without the doctorate. As you investigate doctoral programs, you will discover that there are several types of degrees from which you may choose. The most prominent of these degrees are the Doctor of Philosophy degree (Ph.D.), the Doctor of Education degree (Ed.D.), the Doctor of Arts degree (D.A.), and the Doctor of Physical Education degree (P.E.D. or D.P.E.). These degree programs are based on varying philosophies, principles, and emphases, and curricula may vary widely from institution to institution. An investigation of specific programs will be necessary for you to comprehend fully the scope and intent of the degree offered by a particular institution. Regardless of the degree or the institution that you select, the rewards of graduate study at the doctoral level are well worth the effort, energy, and perseverance necessary to attain the degree.

Education is a dynamic process and is never terminated, even though the doctorate is considered the terminal degree. Your education may be continued through attendance at professional workshops, conventions, and conferences, through memberships in professional organizations, and through numerous other professional endeavors. In addition, there are many postdoctoral programs designed to help you enhance your effectiveness and improve your teaching capabilities. All educators, regardless of the degrees they earn, are obligated to stay abreast of current professional trends, issues, and developments, and to strive constantly to improve the state of the art.

Sports journalism—a challenging field.

ALTERNATIVE CAREERS

As you mature and develop professionally, you may decide that teaching or coaching in the school setting is not your "cup of tea." Fortunately, there are numerous other areas in which you may utilize the skills and knowledges acquired through a physical education professional preparation program. The nature of physical education professional preparation is such that graduates of these programs are usually equipped to make valuable contributions in professions outside the realm of the traditional educational setting. In Table 2, you will find brief descriptions of 10 professions that a physical educator might pursue. Additional possibilities include a career as a sports team manager, sports facilities manager, fitness and health spa instructor, senior citizen recreation coordinator, aquatics specialist, dancer, choreographer, camp director or counselor, military recreation specialist, or adapted physical education specialist. Professional preparation in physical education can be the initial step in becoming qualified to pursue these, and additional, specialties.

Table 2. Ten career choices in physical education and sport

Occupation	Brief job description	Recommended educational preparation	Compensation range*	Occupational outlook*
Athletic trainer	Works in schools and colleges or with professional athletic teams in the prevention and care of injuries associated with competitive athletics	College preparation in curriculum approved by the National Athletic Trainers Association and National Certification Examination	Schools: $7,000-12,000 Professional Teams: $12,000-25,000	Good
Sports official	Employed by schools, colleges, sport clubs and recreation departments to conduct athletic contests in all sports; those with outstanding ability may be eligible for assignment to professional contests	Training and qualifying examination in each sport; must hold membership in officials' organization for each sport.	Clubs, schools, recreation depts.: $10-50 per contest Professional: $50-500 per contest	Good
Professional athlete	Plays baseball, football, basketball, hockey, softball, track and field, tennis, golf, skates or bowls before paying audiences	High school, college for most sports; intensive coaching and practice	$2,500-100,000+	Very few opportunities, heavy competition
Recreation leader	Organizes and directs leisure activities in public agencies, parks and institutions (e.g., YMCA, Scouting, churches, etc.) and corporations; works with part-time and volunteer workers and supervises their training and activities	2-4 year college degree in recreation and/or related fields	$7,500-15,000	Fair

From a flyer developed by the National Association for Sport and Physical Education, National Association for Girls and Women in Sport of the American Alliance for Health, Physical Education, and Recreation. Reprinted by permission of The American Alliance for Health, Physical Education, Recreation and Dance, Washington, D.C.
*Variations in compensation and occupational outlook (availability) depend on geographic area. Occupational outlook and salary estimates realistically reflect employment conditions through 1980.

Table 2. Ten career choices in physical education and sport—cont'd

Occupation	Brief job description	Recommended educational preparation	Compensation range	Occupational outlook
Physical education teacher	Prepares lesson plans and tests, works with students evaluating skills, sportsmanship, effort and participation Position available with preschool through adult levels	College degrees and appropriate teaching credentials	$8,000-25,000	Fair
Athletic coach	Coaches team or individual sports; may specialize in one sport or one aspect of a sport plan, organize practice sessions and strategy; may teach P.E., health or other subjects; makes business arrangements; gives press interviews Opportunities exist in schools, colleges, community and professional sports	College degree with credits in physical education, education and coaching techniques	$300 (part-time) to $75,000+	Excellent for part-time, fair for full-time
Sports journalist or photographer	Works with all media in interpreting the sports world to the public through written, oral or visual communication Opportunities exist at local or big city newspapers, T.V., radio stations, magazines, or as sports information director at colleges or universities	College degree with credits in communications Sports experience helpful Photography experience	$6,000-30,000+	Good

Continued.

Table 2. Ten career choices in physical education and sport—cont'd

Occupation	Brief job description	Recommended educational preparation	Compensation range	Occupational outlook
Sporting goods dealer	Sells sporting goods or manages a department or store; is in charge of purchasing and marketing, supervises office employees and sales personnel; may represent a manufacturer	College degree or management training programs Sports experience helpful	$9,000-25,000+	Excellent
Physical therapist	Works with patients who have been physically disabled through birth, illness or accident; evaluates physiological functions and selects therapeutic procedures for treatment	College degree and state licensing	$8,000-25,000	Good
Physical education and/or athletic administrator	Organizes and supervises competitive and/or instructional programs in clubs, schools, colleges and professional sports; has responsibility for transportation, budget, facilities, personnel, equipment, scheduling and community relations; PE administrator develops curriculum; athletic director participates in fund raising	College degrees with credits in administration Experience in education and athletics helpful	$10,000-30,000+	Good

Sporting goods—a booming business.

The readings associated with this chapter will provide you with information relative to numerous career opportunities, which these articles explore in depth. An examination of them would be valuable in your investigation of alternative careers. In addition, you will discover that articles of this nature are appearing with increasing frequency in professional literature. Public and professional awareness of the capabilities of physical education graduates is growing daily, and maintaining contact with the current developments that are reported in the literature is essential to availing yourself of the most recent and most relevant information.

A better understanding of alternative career opportunities should enable you to determine those careers that are most compatible with your personality, interests, and aptitudes. An investigation of the facts presented in the literature supplemented by discussions with your peers, teachers, and advisers may help you select the career in which you will be able to make the most valuable contributions and from which you will derive the greatest measure of satisfaction. This purposeful approach to your profession should provide you with the information necessary for you to make intelligent, realistic decisions about the career that you may wish to pursue for a lifetime.

SUMMARY

Numerous professional opportunities await you when you become a physical education graduate. Among these opportunities are teaching and coaching, pursuing graduate study, and entering into one of a variety of alternative careers.

As you embark on your professional preparation program and begin to become aware of the many possibilities available, you will also become aware of the many decisions that you must make in preparation for your career. In order for you to make the most prudent decisions, it will be essential for you to conduct thorough investigations of the careers in which you are interested and to attempt correlating the requirements of those careers with your personal goals and aptitudes. Armed with this knowledge, you will be better equipped to plan your professional preparation experiences with a view toward achieving the education and the expertise necessary for you to function most effectively in the career of your choice.

---

1   WHAT TO DO WHEN UNEMPLOYED*

By Elizabeth Noyes
Stamford, Connecticut

The typical physical education instructor, out of a job, is a very restless and dissatisfied person. Whether she is fresh from training school or a veteran of long experience, she has a habit and a tradition of activity and responsibility. Without occupation, she becomes depressed; without exercise, morose. However, being a person of initiative, she generally manages to find something to do. All too frequently this something is a purely financial expedient, with no constructive bearing on her professional or personal objectives. The financial aspect cannot, of course, be disregarded—it will often be necessary to work in a store or in an office—and she will be lucky to get a paying position—but she should make every effort to keep in touch with her profession and to enlarge her experience in it. This period of unemployment can become a post-graduate course in the larger aspects of physical education, instead of a gradual slipping into a more immediately profitable, if less fundamentally satisfying career.

From my own experience, and that of several of my friends, I have gathered a surprisingly (to me, at least) long list of projects in the field of physical education, to which the unemployed trained woman can make a valuable contribution. Her background makes her a very valuable member of any community; and, at the same time, she is given by the community opportunity to practice and brush up on her teaching methods and practical skills, and to enjoy all the physical benefits of her profession.

Perhaps the simplest problem for her to solve is also the most immediate one—that of getting exercise. As she is used to a variety of forms of activity, she may be a little disappointed to have her choice limited to hiking and tennis, but she will not be in the sad state of her neighbor who must have badminton or nothing. As a matter of fact most places nowadays offer a fair variety of sports at a low cost. The big cities are, of course, the worst places in this respect, but they partially make up for lack of ice ponds, golf links, and baseball diamonds by a larger number of gymnasia and pools. One Y.W.C.A. has several volunteer life guards, who are paid through the

*From The Journal of Health and Physical Education **5:**11, 63, March 1934.

medium of free use of the pool and gymnasium facilities, and probably other institutions would be glad to make similar arrangements. Most places of any size have basketball leagues, and often many other sports are similarly organized. And, if a favorite sport is being neglected by a locality, one enthusiast is often sufficient to start a group in it.

Actual teaching experience is harder to get on a volunteer basis. Probably the settlement houses are the best places for this, and the board of recreation activities offer good opportunities for coaches and referees in the various sports. Sometimes it is possible to form classes in popular activities, such as tap dancing or reducing exercises. Playground work, girl scout troops, and life-guarding at the beaches may seem far removed from the days of lesson plans with major and minor objectives, but they give excellent practice in informal teaching methods, as well as a vista of the possibilities and fascination of the recreation field, which is so closely allied to ours, and so frequently neglected by us. The whole field of volunteer social work, especially in the "character-building" organizations, is rich in opportunities for leadership in activities related to physical education. Informal games, outing activities, and dancing are only a few of the items on the programs of these organizations, and volunteers adequately trained to lead these activities are made very welcome by the overworked staff members, and given free rein to develop their own ideas. I know of no case where the schools have used volunteer teachers, but it seems possible that they might, especially in an activity which the regular teacher was not equipped to handle, such as fencing, or corrective gymnastics. Other possibilities in the field of corrective gymnastics include the hospitals, special schools, visiting nurses, and doctors. Pediatricians and gynecologists are often glad to know of someone to whom they can turn over cases of functional poor posture, dysmenorrhea, etc., for supervised exercise, or of someone who could run a clinic for them.

If the unemployed instructor is so situated that she can do graduate study, this may solve her problem; but there are many who have not this opportunity, and who would yet like to keep on learning. For these, it is often possible to take up the study of some related useful accomplishment or hobby. The ability to type, play the piano, lead singing, cook outdoors, make a poster or a costume, or swing an axe, will often be an asset to a teacher of physical education; and so will knowledge of social dance steps, nature lore, science, psychology, art, and music, and most of these activities are available through the resources of even the smaller towns. Typewriters can be borrowed, libraries ransacked, pianos tuned, and experts beguiled into revealing to the earnest inquirer the secrets of their trade and sources of further information. In these and many other ways, new accomplishments which will be of lasting value and pleasure may be acquired.

Perhaps none of these activities I have listed sounds like a full-time job, but a combination of them can make for a very busy life. My own case is an example. During this winter, I have run a girl scout troop and a Girl Reserve club; I have guarded a pool, and received diving lessons in exchange; I have learned to type; had a private pupil for corrective exercises; studied general science and psychology; and planned a playground for the C.W.A. I have earned very little money, but I feel that the year has not been wasted so far. In fact, I have several other projects which I hope to accomplish before the summer. So I feel very strongly that a time of unemployment need not be a complete disaster, but can prove instead a great opportunity to discover and make use of one's own undeveloped talents and interests, and the resources of one's community. The activities which I have mentioned do not by any means cover the field of possibilities—many others will be suggested by an individual's own interests and situation. But it is hoped that even this incomplete survey may be of some constructive assistance, not only to my fellow idlers, but to the various agencies which might be able to use their services and help them in their professional efforts.

2   SOME POSSIBILITIES FOR EMPLOYMENT IN PHYSICAL EDUCATION'S ALLIED FIELDS*

By James E. Bryant
Associate Professor of Physical Education at Metropolitan State College, Denver

Physical education majors are limited in scope as to what professions are open to them upon graduation. Today's job market is now vastly limited in the area of physical education teaching throughout the country. Students must be exceptional in their field and then be willing to move to remote rural areas to accept a teaching position. It is the purpose of this article to inform students in physical education of the possibilities and potentialities for employment in physical education and its allied fields.

The field of teaching physical education in public schools. The trends in physical education are directed toward teachers with a background in aquatics, gymnastics, life-time sports and coed teaching for both men and women at the secondary level. Women who have a strong coaching background and skill in athletic training are also in demand to a degree. Men are still much in need at the elementary level of physical education and, in fact, still don't have to be extremely mobile to find a position. Teaching minors that are helpful for the secondary major are: art, music, biology, and math. Surprisingly, history is a resurging minor that at least provides the graduate with an area to apply for a position regardless of the number of applicants.

Physical therapy field. The physical education major still is highly qualified in the area of physical therapy providing he has a strong background in the sciences. With a graduate degree he can find a good position with less effort than it takes to enter the teaching field. Recreation therapy is a related direction the physical educator can go with great employment success without having quite so extensive a background in biology.

Recreation field. Fewer individuals are now accepted in private or community recreation with a major in physical education although many still find their way into this field providing they have a

recreation minor. In fact, it still is easier to enter community recreation as a specialist in physical activity than to find a teaching position.

Specialist fields. One of the most wide open fields today is in the area of private physical education specialists. A list of these is found below:

1. Tennis specialists (tennis pro, country club lessons, playing on pro tennis circuit)
2. Golf specialists (golf club pro, playing on pro golf circuit)
3. Aquatic specialists (swimming pool manager, private swimming lessons)
4. Bowling specialists (bowling pro shop manager, pro bowling circuit)
5. Skiing specialists (ski lessons resort areas, pro ski circuit)
6. Ice skating specialists (ice skating rink manager, private ice skating lessons)

Each of these areas requires a physical education background and a certain degree of skill in the particular specialty. A business minor or major is also an excellent choice for a major or minor.

Other specialists related areas include:

1. Golf course architect and maintenance
2. Tennis court construction and salesman
3. Swimming pool construction and maintenance
4. Resort manager for skiing

These specialty areas require various backgrounds that would include interest in physical education. Again, a business background is important as is possibly an advertisement background.

College teaching or college athletics field. Several potential physical education related areas are found at the college level. With advanced degrees (M.S., Ed.D. or Ph.D.) students are qualified to teach at the college level. Junior colleges are still an important phase of college education and teaching at this level along with coaching is still a strong possibility. Working with intramural programs at the college or university

*From The Physical Educator **31**:193-195, December 1974.

level provides opportunities. For some students research in the areas of tests and measurements in physical education, kinesiology, and exercise physiology is advantageous. Hybrid areas of adaptive physical education (a combination of physical education and special education) are open fields of research.

Athletics offers outstanding opportunity for involvement at the college level. These fields include: athletic business manager, athletic publicity director, and athletic trainer. Business managers, of course, need to have a background in business along with an athletic or physical education background. Publicity directors need a media background in journalism, television, radio, and advertisement to match expertise in physical education or athletics. The athletic trainer is subject to an advanced degree with emphasis toward physical therapy and certification as a trainer by NATA (National Athletic Trainers Association). The athletic trainer probably would be involved in some college teaching—particularly care and prevention of athletic injuries.

Professional sports field. Professional sports offers a fabulous but limited field of professional growth. For an athlete, professional athletics including: baseball, basketball, football, soccer, ice hockey, golf, and tennis are all lucrative. Tennis, above all, is a wide open field for employment.

Physical education majors with athletic backgrounds often can become involved with professional sports as a: business manager, publicity director, athletic trainer, equipment manager, official, ticket sales manager, and scout. The business manager, ticket sales manager, publicity director, or trainer need backgrounds similar to their college counterparts, but no special preparation is needed for the other areas except an athletic background.

Media field. Radio and television sports casting offer beautiful opportunities for the physical education graduate with a speech and/or journalism preparation. Sports writing in national magazines or local newspapers offer opportunities for the individual with a journalism background. Media needs people with the expertise in physical education or athletics along with journalism and/or speech.

Private physical education related organizations. YMCA and YWCA organizations are constantly looking for young men and women with majors in physical education. Possible promotions to physical fitness or activities directors make these organizations financially worthwhile

for the person with a degree. Boy's clubs and girl's clubs are another possibility as they relate to the Y programs. Although not as professionally oriented, martial arts (Tae Kwan Do, Judo, Karate, and Kung Fu) is a rapidly expanding field of profitable business. Health clubs too are not considered professionally oriented but a background in physical education is an asset in the business and possibly would provide a more ethical representation for these clubs.

Sporting goods field. With the tremendous influx of sports involvement by the public, the physical education graduate has an excellent opportunity in the sporting goods business as either a local sporting goods dealer or as a sports company representative. Companies such as: Rawlings, Wilson, Champion, E. R. Moore, and Converse All Star are always in the market for bright young people with a physical education background and an interest in athletics.

Miscellaneous fields. There are numerous fields not yet discussed that are briefly listed with comments below:

1. Art form of physical education—an individual combining art talents with a physical education degree can become involved with private art enterprise in the area of physical movement or in commercial art with sports cover page layouts, etc.

2. Publication companies in physical education including W. B. Saunders, Prentice-Hall, and Wm. C. Brown all have openings in sales for knowledgeable people in athletics and physical education.

3. International sports interpreter with a background combination of physical education and languages and a degree of good fortune could possibly represent the United States teams overseas at international events.

Conclusion. As can be readily observed, there are 45-50 separate professions listed above that are related to physical education to some degree. Many other professions could possibly be added to the list providing even a greater scope of related fields for the new graduate in physical education. All those connected with the major in physical education have a responsibility to inform him of opportunities in and out of teaching. Students need to be made aware of challenging opportunities available to them and not be channeled automatically to an already glutted field of teaching physical education. Students need to know all possibilities for employment in physical education's allied fields.

3 THE PHYSICAL EDUCATOR AS TEACHER*

By Celeste Ulrich**

Teaching is a reciprocal. It is incomplete unless there be learning, for it is a paired cross between scholar and mentor. Teaching is a handshake, with all of the implications that such a gesture implies. Teaching is the offering and the acceptance of trust, understanding, respect, knowledge and challenge. The teacher says, "and there's a hand my trusty fiere"; the student considers the consequences "and gie's a hand o'thine." The pact is sealed. Never is life the same again for either teacher or student.

The consequences of such a pact are manifold. They tinge the lives of all involved with the responsibility of education. The consequences cast an aura of intimate concern for individuals, for society, and for universals. The consequences are so poignant that it is a wonder that anyone would dare to chance such a relationship, that anyone would dare to teach. Yet, the world is full of teachers and students, and the awe of the relationship is tempered by the commonality of the experience.

Physical educators are first and foremost teachers. They must teach, for theirs is the charge of trust, understanding, respect, knowledge and challenge through the handshake which claims human mobility as its unique characteristic. Mobility is a reasonable charge and physical educators reason by teaching.

The Greeks, who suggested logic as a method

of reason, believed that logic involved the concepts of *men* ($\mu\acute{\epsilon}\nu$), meaning "on the hand," and of *de* ($\delta\acute{\epsilon}$), meaning "on the other hand." Such was the balance which reason demanded. The teacher must employ such logic when reasoning about his role. The physical educator, as a teacher, should logically see himself in reasonable balance.

"On one hand" teaching offers many positive values. The opportunity to dedicate oneself to an idea, an ideal, and an ideology is a satisfying and meaningful experience. Dedication carries the implication of service, and usually of service to mankind. Such dedication is heady potion for any individual.

"On one hand" there are the material benefits of teaching. Although such benefits are the subject of derision, they exist and they are desirable. There are decent working hours, respectable facilities, livable working wages, rich cultural opportunities, desirable personal associations and even a multitude of two and three day holidays with a grandiose three month vacation for self enrichment—albeit that it is usually without pay. The material benefits of teaching suggest affluence, even when the affluence is not reflected in financial gain.

"On one hand" there is the cooperative concept of the teaching reciprocal. It is a shared endeavor with people anxious to assist each other. There is little of the "dog eat dog" attitude in teaching. Ideas are common property, methods are mutual adventures of cooperation.

"On one hand" there is the status of the teaching-learning reciprocal. Even the "egghead" has mien which demands respect in spite of the "other worldliness" of scholarly dispositions. The teacher may be teased, taunted, or even pitied, but the teacher is never ignored. In the United States the teacher commands tempered respect and admiration, for education is the vehicle of social mobility and the teacher is the conductor of such a vehicle.

But, "on the other hand," teaching has liabilities and the intelligent physical educator must see the balance of both hands. For, "on the other

---

*From Quest **7:**58-61, December 1966.

**About the Author.* Celeste Ulrich, Ph.D., is Professor of Physical Education at The Woman's College of the University of North Carolina. Dr. Ulrich is also known to the profession as an author and as a forthright speaker. After years of service in the Southern Association for Physical Education of College Women and on various national committees, Celeste Ulrich assumed the presidency of N.A.P.E.C.W. in July, 1965. A noteworthy teacher with a following of students in Oregon, Colorado and Michigan, Dr. Ulrich writes about the physical educator as teacher from a broad experiential base. To fit the format of the publication, the title she proposed for her article was changed from "And There's A Hand." It seems most appropriate to include Dr. Ulrich's first contribution to *Quest* in this issue.

hand," there is the journey of loneliness which usually accompanies any search for ultimate meanings. There are no teachers to whom the master teacher can turn, and teaching is a lonely, personalized adventure. There are friends, and colleagues, and students, but essentially the teacher is alone with his thoughts, his perceptions, and his decisions.

"On the other hand" teaching involves anxiety; it spawns anxiety, it perpetuates anxiety, it feeds on anxiety. There is the anxiety of "not knowing," the anxiety of "coping and adaptation," the anxiety of "autonomy." Teaching does not foster serenity and tranquility and the "ivory tower" atmosphere in education, if it ever really existed, existed only in the concept that "understood anxiety" has a virtue. In an anxious world, with anxious people, the teacher is among the most anxious. He is anxious because anxiety produces change and education fosters change.

"On the other hand" teaching must contend with hostility. There is hostility to ignorance, hostility to authority, hostility to conformity, hostility to anarchy. The social process of conflict is as readily employed by teachers as that of cooperation. Hostility drains the emotional reserve of the teacher for it usurps energy and debilitates commitment.

"On the other hand" teaching is an escape. It is an escape into a world which has boundaries and rules which are overtly established and easily ascertained. It is an escape from the exasperation of ignorance and stupidity, from a world only concerned with outcomes and seldom caring about methods. Teaching can be an escape from function and reality, from a relative atmosphere. Teaching can permit escape to a world of ideated absolutes. Teaching can be unreal.

Thus, it is apparent that the reciprocal of teaching is always balanced by the *men* and the *de* and such balance must be reasoned by the physical educator as a teacher.

But having resolved the turmoil of decision making, having found a *men-de* balance, having resolved to participate in an educational hand clasp; what are the characteristics and description of the teaching reciprocal's excellence?

Fundamentally, the teacher must possess knowledge and believe in the worth of such knowledge. Such a fundamental has been generally ignored with regard to physical education. Physical educators have been interested too long in the personality of the teacher and the concomitants of the subject matter, with resulting

neglect of knowledge *about* the subject and a lack of understanding about the worth of such knowledge. Although mathematicians know that changing a dollar bill utilizes concepts of the decimal system, they have not committed mathematics to the set of ten because of dollar bills. There are times when physical educators have acted as though the opportunity to know how to play tennis when one is out of school is the most important reason to understand human mobility. No teacher can use method to teach "nothing." There must be "something" to teach. The method can evolve, the subject cannot. Nice people who like to play and who get along with other people are not always good physical educators. There needs to be an understanding of the meaning of human movement and there has to be a belief in the worth of such an idea.

The teacher must possess sincerity. Nothing is more apparent than a lack of sincerity and while one can transmit knowledge without sincerity, one cannot teach without sincerity. There has to be a sincere interest in people, in the subject matter and in the teacher's responsibility to bring together all of these jigsaw facets.

The teacher must accept and believe in humanness, including his own. Teachers are not paragons of virtue nor are they teaching students who are perfected paragons. The very humanity of teaching creates the reciprocal and the good teacher not only accepts the right to be human, he encourages it. A student is not a disciple sitting at the feet of the savior-teacher. A student is a part of the paired cross which makes the magic of the educational handshake both a total entity and a gesture of integrity.

The teacher always has the difficult task of determining the symbolism of the handshake. To be one with the students and not one of them is a nebulous line to draw. Yet, it is in the restriction of a handshake that teaching takes place. Teaching is not adoration, although there is adoration in teaching. Teaching is not friendship although there is friendship in teaching. Teaching is not respect although there is respect in teaching. Teaching insists upon rules of conduct which are essential for the maintenance of integrity. The establishment of such rules is determined by tradition, propriety, decorum and the good sense of the teacher.

Teaching demands industry and will power. The industry of continual elaboration of ideas is demanding work. It is so much simpler to teach this year, as you taught last year, as you taught the year before. To continue to be innovative with regard to subject matter is difficult. It takes will power. Industry and will power are manifested also in remembering to treat students as individuals and not as waves which ebb and flood over the same strand for generation upon generation.

It takes industry and will power to act as if the handshake is a new experience for the people involved—which indeed it is. Teachers dare not cultivate the "receiving line hand" with its limp fish feeling when they venture to shake the hand of a generation of students.

Teachers have to have a sense of humor. There has to be a touch of the whimsical, an ability to chuckle at the problems of reality, a desire not to take one's self or subject matter so seriously that the absurdity of reality and the inaneness of ideas are missed. A sense of humor serves the teaching reciprocal well. It strengthens the bond of understanding and makes light the heavy heart and the weighty world.

And above all, teachers must be real. They must possess compassion and empathy and understanding even as they lack such qualities. They must care and they must be unfeeling, they must have faith and they must have facts, they must be tolerant and they must be demanding; they must be very much whatever they are. And they must have love.

Teaching is not love, but teaching without love is not teaching. The teacher must love people and ideas and life and in so doing, he dares to offer the hand. In the offering of the most intimate core of self, the teacher must know that there are times when the hand will be rejected, when the grip will be too firm or too loose, when the clasp will be insincere, when the shake will hurt. Yet, in spite of these understandings and because of them, the physical educator will dare to teach because he loves.

The physical educator loves movement, he loves his responsibility for people, he loves his devotion to an idea, he loves the concept of service, and he loves the process which permits all of these kaleidoscopic parts to assume a meaningful pattern. The physical educator loves to teach.

The physical educator is many things to many people in many situations. He is a scholar, he is an advisor, he is a coach, he is an artist, he is a researcher, he is an administrator, he is an evaluator, he is an author. Yet in all of these varied roles, he is *always* a teacher. He is a teacher because that is his essence, that is his commitment, that is his love.

With all of the integrity of his being, the physical educator chooses to dare to teach. He extends himself and his disciplines when turning to a student he says, "and there's a hand my trusty fiere, and gie's a hand o' thine." There is glory and promise in that reciprocal.

SUPPLEMENTAL READINGS
1950-1959

4. Harnett, Arthur L., Jr.: Career information for high schools, Journal of Health, Physical Education, and Recreation **28**:25-26, December 1957.

1960-1969

5. Bischoff, David C.: The physical educator as administrator, Quest **7**:14-17, December 1966.
6. Fraleigh, Warren P.: The perplexed professor, Quest **7**:1-13, December 1966.
7. Governali, Paul: The physical educator as coach, Quest **7**:30-33, December 1966.
8. Gray, Miriam: The physical educator as artist, Quest **7**:18-24, December 1966.
9. Hartman, Betty G.: Training women to coach, Journal of Health, Physical Education, and Recreation **39**:25, 76, January 1968.
10. Huelster, Laura J.: The physical educator in perspective, Quest **7**:62-66, December 1966.
11. Massey, Benjamin H.: The physical educator as researcher, Quest **7**:46-52, December 1966.
12. Mordy, Margaret A.: The physical educator as graduate adviser, Quest **7**:34-38, December 1966.
13. Programs for handicapped, Journal of

Health, Physical Education, and Recreation **39**:83-84, 86, October 1968.

14. Shaw, John H.: The physical educator as author, Quest **7**:25-29, December 1966.

15. Smithells, Philip A.: The physical educator as professor, Quest **7**:53-57, December 1966.

16. Wilson, Ruth M.: The physical educator as evaluator, Quest **7**:39-45, December 1966.

1970-1979

17. Barry, Pat, Edwards, Emily, and Koenigsberg, Ruth: HPER career preparation for high school students, The Journal of Physical Education and Recreation **46**:45-46, April 1975.

18. Berlin, Pearl: The great conglomerate; graduate education at the master's level, Quest **25**:45-57, Winter 1976.

19. Bullaro, John J.: Career potential in commercial recreation, The Journal of Physical Education and Recreation **46**: 36-37, November-December 1975.

20. Cleland, Donna: Preparing women coaches and athletic administrators, The Journal of Physical Education and Recreation **48**:18-19, October 1977.

21. Cooper, John M.: The pros and cons of graduate education with large enrollments in large universities, Quest **25**: 36-44, Winter 1976.

22. Crase, Darrell: Educated and unwanted; dilemma of the seventies, The Journal of Physical Education and Recreation **47**: 41-42, May 1976.

23. Epperson, Arlin: Opportunities for recreation students in the travel and tourism industry, The Journal of Physical Education and Recreation **46**:38, 48, November-December 1975.

24. Finn, Peter: Career education and physical education, The Journal of Physical Education and Recreation **47**:29-31, January 1976.

25. Fried, David H.: Alternative career opportunities related to physical educa-

tion, The Journal of Physical Education and Recreation **50**:72, January 1979.

26. Johnston, James M.: College teaching; towards a new definition, Quest **25**:25-28, Winter 1976.

27. Lepley, Paul M., and Eastman, W. Dean: Alternative careers for physical educators, The Journal of Physical Education and Recreation **48**:29, January 1977.

28. Leslie, David K., and McLure, John W.: The preparation of physical educators for expanded leadership and service roles, Journal of Health, Physical Education, and Recreation **43**:71, 73, November-December 1972.

29. Parkhouse, Bonnie L.: Professional preparation in athletic administration and sport management, The Journal of Physical Education and Recreation **49**: 22-27, May 1978.

30. Siedentop, Daryl: Graduate education; a conversation with Jonas Soltis, Quest **25**:16-24, Winter 1976.

31. Vinton, Dennis A.: Preparing for careers in the leisure industries; a career education approach, The Journal of Physical Education and Recreation **46**:39-40, November-December 1975.

ASSIGNMENTS
Individual activities

1. Read article 3 and assess your suitability for teaching in light of Dr. Ulrich's viewpoints toward characteristics of teachers.

2. Read article 1 and discuss its implications for modern-day physical education graduates.

3. Utilizing Table 2 (pp. 128-130) and articles in the reading list, investigate one or more of the careers that appeal to you.
   ARTICLES: 1-4, 7, 9, 13, 17, 19, 20, 23-25, 27-29, 31.

4. Invite a guest speaker to class to discuss career possibilities for physical education graduates. Appropriate speakers might be the Director of the Placement Center on your campus or any other in-

dividual involved with career planning for university graduates.

5. Invite a guest panel to conduct a discussion for the class. Members of this panel might include representatives from organizations such as the Young Men's Christian Association, Young Women's Christian Association, Scouts, American National Red Cross, nursing homes, camps, travel agencies, and health spas.

6. Investigate the responsibilities of the college physical educator.
   ARTICLES: 3, 5-8, 10-12, 14-16, 26.

7. Investigate graduate study in physical education.
   ARTICLES: 12, 18, 21, 29, 30.

Group presentations

1. Panel discussion
   a. TOPIC: *Alternative career opportunities.*
   b. PARTICIPANTS: Contemporary physical education major students.
   c. FUNCTIONS: To discuss alternative career opportunities for physical educators.
   d. OBJECTIVES OF PRESENTATION: (1) To identify specific authors and the time periods in which they addressed themselves to the issue, (2) to present and discuss specific alternative career opportunities for physical educators, (3) to indicate recommendations for the improvement of career education, (4) to recognize the consistency of atti-

tudes toward the capabilities of physical educators relative to alternative career possibilities, (5) to entertain questions from class members.
   e. ARTICLES: 1, 2, 4, 7, 9, 13, 17, 19, 20, 22-25, 27-29, 31.

2. Panel discussion
   a. TOPIC: *Graduate study in physical education.*
   b. PARTICIPANTS: Contemporary physical educators.
   c. FUNCTION: To investigate graduate study in physical education.
   d. OBJECTIVES OF PRESENTATION: (1) To identify specific authors, (2) to discuss various aspects of graduate study in physical education.
   e. ARTICLES: 12, 18, 21, 29, 30.

3. Panel discussion
   a. TOPIC: *The roles of the professor of physical education.*
   b. PARTICIPANTS: Contemporary physical educators.
   c. FUNCTION: To present information about the responsibilities of physical educators at the college level.
   d. OBJECTIVES OF PRESENTATION: (1) To identify specific authors; (2) to elaborate on the responsibilities of the physical educator as administrator, artist, author, coach, graduate adviser, evaluator, researcher, scholar, and teacher.
   e. ARTICLES: 3, 5-8, 10-12, 14-16, 26.

Index